CELTIC MYTHS,
CELTIC LEGENDS

Celtic Myths, Celtic Legends

R. J. Stewart

COLOUR ILLUSTRATIONS BY COURTNEY DAVIS

BLANDFORD

A BLANDFORD BOOK

First published 1994
by Blandford, a Cassell imprint
Villiers House
41/47 Strand
London
WC2N 5JE

Distributed in the United States
by Sterling Publishing Co., Inc.
387 Park Avenue South, New York, New York 10016-8810

Distributed in Australia
by Capricorn Link (Australia) Pty Ltd
2/13 Carrington Road, Castle Hill, NSW 2154

British Library Cataloguing-in-Publication Data
A catalogue record for this book is available
from the British Library

ISBN 0-7137-2423-4

Typeset by Litho Link Ltd., Welshpool, Powys, Wales
Printed and bound in Spain by Cronion S.A. Barcelona

Contents

the Colour Illustrations

acknowledgements

'The Game of Chess' in Chapter 9 is reprinted (with some changes) from my *Magical Tales*, first published in 1990 by Aquarian Press. All the other stories are based on sources given in the Bibliography, where they are listed under the relevant chapters.

I would like to acknowledge the advice and generous help of John and Caitlín Matthews and the prodigious typing of Sian Barrie and Julie Timbrell. Inspiration and support came from Robert and Lorraine Henry in Ulster, with visits to ancient sites and sources of Celtic tradition and literature.

The line illustrations were specially drawn for this book by Sarah Lever.

Introduction

This is not a strictly academic set of translations but a wide-ranging collection of themes from Celtic myths and legends. Some of the tales are translated directly from Irish, Breton or Welsh, and some from Latin or medieval French. Others are written anew from ideas or older tales that embody Celtic myths.

The individual items range historically from extracts of early sagas that seem to come from the time of bronze weapons (though not written down by Irish monks until the eighth century) to my own twentieth-century versions of classic Celtic tales. Between these elder and younger voices is a wealth of material from folklore, manuscript, and various books and collections that use Celtic myths in either an academic or an imaginative way. Some of the source texts and academic commentaries are listed in the Bibliography, as are suggestions for further reading into the imaginative power and potential of Celtic tradition.

In *Celtic Gods, Celtic Goddesses* I described some of the major and minor Celtic deities, their attributes, ceremonies and worship, powers and traditions, and the ways in which they might have an inspirational poetic or visionary value for us today. In *Celtic Myths, Celtic Legends* I have gathered tales that seem to carry the Celtic tradition through time, offering something of the beauty and savagery, the spirituality and sensuousness, of the Celtic ancestors and their modern descendants.

There is a tendency in modern revivals of Celtic lore and legend towards prettiness – a falsely romantic approach that conveniently ignores the harsh and often violent nature of Celtic tradition. While I have not hesitated to include some of the more romantic themes, at the same time I have not tried to omit the battles, the vengeance, the cruelty. Without these hard edges, beauty and inspiration can become insipid, and lose its value.

The main sources of material in this collection are as follows:

1 Celtic literature from historically defined collections and manuscripts. These are quoted from various translations, and have been edited or sometimes completely rewritten for this book.
2 Interpretations and reworkings of Celtic myths and legends through the centuries by various writers, also quoted and occasionally rewritten.
3 Folklore, traditional ballads and traditional tales. This third category is an important and often ignored source of Celtic myths and legends, even in the present century.

The book is not, however, arranged in these three categories or sections; rather, the stories are gathered together in an order designed either to contrast or to link with one another, regardless of their varied sources.

Two particular themes emerge from this net of myths and legends. One is the presence or re-emergence of the Great Goddess, known by many names in Celtic tradition, from the blood-drenched Morrighu (Morrigan) to the shining Brigit and the mysterious Queen of Elfland. The other is the paradoxical role of the hero, at once warrior, buffoon and willing sacrifice for all. A third theme, woven in between the other two, is that of love triumphing, sometimes mercilessly, over all opposition.

Celtic tradition and culture, essentially pagan, seem to have provided fertile ground for early Christianity in northern Europe, long before dogmatism and suppression crept in. Many Celtic legends have Christian and pagan themes interlaced: perhaps the most important of these are the Grail texts, and the massive body of Arthurian literature.

The St Andrews
Sarcophagus, Scotland.

Some of this fusion is found in a few of the stories in here, particularly with the idea of the old religion as foster-mother or spiritual parent to the new. This fostering is often repugnant to political religion, but contains a deep insight into the Celtic psyche, which is inclusive and protean rather than dogmatic and rigid.

So, here are some of the adventures of the Celtic gods and goddesses, the queens and powerful women, the heroes, the saints and madmen, the fools and lovers.

Author's Note to the Reader

The spelling and language found in each story

The myths and legends offered here in translation come from a variety of languages and include several variant spellings in any one language; this is particularly true of the Irish sources. I have not attempted to standardize the spellings throughout and nor have I sought one 'pure' spelling in preference to any others. Readers should simply enjoy the legend, taking the names at face value as they are found in each story.

There is a tendency in some of the older translations of Celtic texts to use a medieval 'courtly' tone, including phrases and words that were not in the originals, as such English-language conventions had not developed at the time of the tales' transformations from oral Celtic languages into written Latin, Irish, Gaelic, Breton, French and so forth. In some cases I have simplified and edited this genteel or antiquarian approach and modernized the text; in others I have let it remain. The reader, though, needs to be aware that the medieval courtly ambience of certain stories is purely an invention of the original translator. In some sources, however (such as *The Mabinogion*), there is a rich mixture of true medieval with ancient Welsh and Irish poetic or bardic conventions, themes and phrases, as these tales were first written down in the medieval period, even though they were drawn from a much older stratum of story-telling.

The black and white illustrations

The drawings located throughout the book show a variety of sites and artefacts connected with Celtic tradition, and many are specifically Celtic, ranging from Bronze Age items through to the art of the Celtic early Christian Church. Some are of megalithic sites and objects, predating the Celts by many years but playing a strong role in Celtic myths and legends through the centuries.

1 bran and branwen

(Wales)

The Mabinogion, from which this tale of Bran and Branwen is adapted, is a major source of Celtic myths and legends from Welsh tradition. Though much of the indigenous culture of Wales and many of its tradition were ruthlessly suppressed by English rule, *The Mabinogion* demonstrates the richness and complexity of the ancient tales preserved in oral tradition by bards or story-tellers. There are eleven stories in all, written down from oral tradition in two collections: *Llyfr Gwyn Rhydderch* (The White Book of Rhydderch), dated between 1300 and 1325, and *Llyfr Coch Hergest* (The Red Book of Hergest), dated between 1375 and 1425. The White Book is in the National Library of Wales at Aberystwyth, with several earlier manuscripts (MSS Peniarth 6, 7, 14, 16) which also contain material from *The Mabinogion*. The Red Book is in the Library of Jesus College, Oxford. The medieval dates of the manuscripts relate only to when the traditional stories were written down: the stories themselves are actually centuries older.

Scholars can date the language and social customs of some of the tales to the eleventh century or earlier, but the mythic themes have their roots in pre-Christian Celtic culture, at least a thousand years before the medieval scribes were working upon their vellum.

The name *Mabinogion* was coined by Lady Charlotte Guest in the nineteenth century, and her translation has been used as the basis for this retelling. Modern scholars, however, have suggested that her title for the collection of tales was based on a linguistic error, as she assumed *Mabinogion* was the plural of *Mabinogi*, meaning youthful adventures (from *mab*, youth). In *Mabon and the Mysteries of Britain*, Caitlin Matthews puts forward the idea that the adventures were originally the quest for the divine child Mabon, who is sought by the Arthurian heroes in the story of 'Culhwch and Olwen'. The name Mabon appears in Romano-Celtic inscriptions, and he is also known as Mabon son of Modron, which simply means 'Son of the Mother'. The idea behind the quest for the absent Mabon is both simple and profound: to find the child we pass through all the orders of created life one by one, until he or she is discovered at the centre of existence.

In the story from *The Mabinogion* which follows, we encounter a legend of the Celtic Titans. Bran and Branwen are ancestral or titanic beings, in the world before humans, and are of gigantic stature by comparison. Bran is the guardian of Britain, and after his death his sacred head is buried on what is now the site of the Tower of London, as magical protection for the land.

---

bRAN the son of Llyr was crowned King of the Island of Britain, and with his family and royal court he travelled from London to Wales. One afternoon they were at Harlech in Ardudwy, and sat upon a cliff looking out over the sea towards Ireland. They were at Branwen's Tower, and there was Bran son of Llyr, his sister Branwen, his half-brother Manawyddan and many more in the court of Bran. They saw thirteen ships sailing from unseen Ireland, and sent men to hail them as they approached the shore.

In the ships were Matholwch, King of Ireland, and his companions, come to ask Bran for Branwen, for Matholwch wished to have her as his queen. The Irish and the Welsh agreed to meet together in Aberffraw, upon the sacred island of Anglesey, and there the ceremonies would take place. The Irish travelled to Anglesey in their ships, over the waves, while the Welsh travelled on horseback, over the land, crossing when the tidé was low. There was no house that could hold Bran the Blessed, so the entire company set up a camp of tents at Aberffraw, and Branwen and Matholwch were joined with due ritual and lay together.

Manawyddan had two half-brothers from his mother's first marriage, before she was with Llyr his father. These sons of Penardun, mother of Manawyddan, were called Nissyen and Evnissyen. Nissyen was a bringer of peace, but Evnissyen was a bringer of strife. Thinking that he should have been consulted over the matter of Branwen's marriage to the King of Ireland, and angry that his consent had not been asked, and feeling slighted and bitter, Evnissyen took his sharpest knife and set off to where the Irish had tethered their best horses. He cut off the tails, the lips, and the ears and eyebrows of Matholwch's horses, causing great outrage and insult and strife.

Such was the rage of the Irish king that Bran hardly knew how to appease him, but he offered him great gifts. Every horse was replaced with a fine new one, and to Matholwch Bran gave a huge golden disc as broad as the king's face, and tall silver staff as high as the king's height.

'I will do more,' said Bran, 'for I shall give you a cauldron that came originally from Ireland, and its power is that if any dead man is put into it he will come back to life, but he will have lost the power of speech.'

The Story of the Cauldron

The second evening that the Irish and the Britons sat down together after the compensation had been settled, Matholwch asked Bran where he had obtained the Cauldron of Regeneration.

'It came to me,' said Bran, 'from a man who had been in Ireland, and I think that he found it there.'

'What was the name of this cauldron-finder?' asked Matholwch.

'Llaser Llaes Gyfnewid, from Ireland, and with him came his wife, Cymedei Cymeinfoll. They fled to Britain after they escaped from an iron house that had been made red hot all around them to kill them. My guess is that you know more of this tale than I do.'

'Indeed I do,' replied Matholwch, ready to tell the full story now that the required preliminary circumlocutions were completed. 'And I will tell you all of it. One day, in Ireland, I was out hunting upon a sacred mound that overlooks a lake. It was a place where only a king may hunt, and the lake is called the Lake of the Cauldron. As I stood upon that hill,

Bronze Celtic cauldron, found in Kincardine Moss, Scotland.

as alone as a king surely is when he has only his huntsmen, his scouts, his personal war-band and the druid of the day all about him, I saw a wonder. Alone as I was, I saw a big monstrous yellow-red-haired man come up out of the lake, bearing a cauldron upon his back. He had the shifty look of a powerful thief about him, and if he was big, the woman that came with him was twice as big as he, and three times as ugly, shifty and thieving. They strode up to me, seeing how alone I was upon the sacred mound, and, easier to reach and converse with than ever a king should be, they boldly greeted me as equals, asking me how I fared in that place.

'And how fares it with you?' I replied, using the common tongue for fear that they might not understand me without my heralds, bards, poets and speechmakers to intervene between us.

'It's like this, high lord,' bellowed the man, and his breath fairly parted the whiskers upon my face. 'This woman, magnificent and wholesome, will conceive after one moon and fourteen more nights have been counted. And she will bear a son out of her bursting, fecund womb, and he will be nothing less than a fully armed warrior.'

Gold sceptre or staff ornament.

Well, as was required of me by the laws of hospitality, which even a solitary and virtually unattended king out hunting alone and lonely must obey, sacred as these laws are, I took the hideous huge couple back with me and maintained them. Indeed, I kept them for one twelve-month, a full year, and in that time they were loud and large, but no one begrudged them the due hospitality. But after the year had passed, and at the end of the first third of the next year, which was as Beltane approached, they had made themselves unwelcome and hated throughout the land. They harassed and molested chieftains and their wives as if such nobles were only slaves or servants, and this the slaves and servants particularly objected to, for the foul and fat man and his fouler and fatter wife were demolishing all precedent and tradition. Indeed, the entire people rose up and offered me the usual choice offered to an all-powerful king wedded to the sovereign land, which was to do what they demanded or be ploughed in.

So I took advice from the full tribal assembly, even though their genealogies took a further fortnight to recite before anyone could make a suggestion. The giant couple would not leave willingly, and it was impossible for us to force them, as their fighting power was as strong as their breath. The assembly decided to make a huge house of iron, and when it was ready every smith and everyone owning tongs and hammers in the whole of the five provinces of Ireland was summoned to the place where the house was.

Now the woman, the man and their warrior offspring were lured into the iron house with a shocking amount of meat and strong drink. Meanwhile, men and women were piling charcoal all around and about and over that house, and when the giants were thoroughly glutted and roaringly drunk, the charcoal was set alight with a tiny wee fire of twigs. Then the army of bellows-blowers set to work until the charcoal mountain glowed yellow then red, and until the iron house became white hot. Inside the giants held a council in the very centre of the house where all directions meet, and when the walls were at their softest and the heat was at its hardest, the man ran at the wall and thrust his massive shoulder into it and broke out. The woman lumbered after him, but only the original two escaped. And I suppose it was after their escape that they came to Britain and to you.'

'Indeed, and the man gave me that very cauldron which I have now given to you,' said Bran.

'And how did you treat these people?' asked Matholwch.

'As their numbers grew, I quartered them throughout the realm, in all of the Four Directions. Now they are numerous, and found everywhere, and wherever they settle they fortify that place with warriors and arms, and they are the best fighting allies that have ever been seen.'

Matholwch was silent for a while, as if weighing the value of the cauldron against the loss of such powerful allies. But as the night wore on they drank and sang and celebrated, and in the morning thirteen ships set sail for Ireland, and Matholwch aboard the finest, and Branwen with him.

When nine months were past Branwen gave birth to a son, and he was called Gwern. As was the custom, Gwern was fostered among the high-ranking warrior families of Ireland.

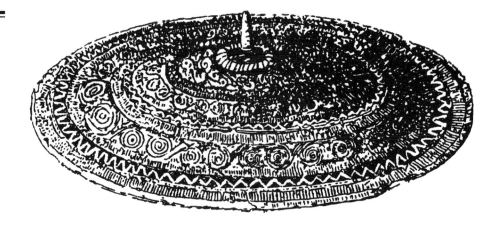

When Branwen had been in Ireland for one year, and coming into her second year as queen to Matholwch's king, the rumour of the maimed horses reached the people of the land. Matholwch's foster-brothers and blood relations who had not been in Wales demanded that Branwen must atone for the insult and the mutilation of the royal horses.

Branwen was forced to work in the kitchen, and every day the butcher who cut up the meat was ordered to hit her upon the side of her head and box her ear. While this was being done to Branwen, all travelling and messages between Ireland and Britain ceased for three years, for fear that Bran might hear of the cruel treatment of his sister. But Branwen was cunning, and she tamed a starling, teaching it to speak. She tied a letter to the starling's wing, and bid it fly over the sea to Wales and find her brother, the King of Britain.

When the starling landed on Bran's shoulder, it ruffled its wings and revealed the letter from Branwen, which was no sooner seen than read. When he discovered the news of his sister's ill-treatment at the Irish court, Bran raised a vast army from among his allies in one hundred and fifty countries. When this host was assembled, and provisioned, and armed, and aboard a huge fleet of ships, Bran gave the care of Britain into the hands of his son Caradawc and seven companions, and set off for Ireland, wading through the sea, for no ship could contain him.

As the swineherds of King Matholwch herded their pigs near the shore, they saw something wondrous and strange. There was a forest upon the sea, and with it a mountain with a high ridge and a lake on each side of the ridge. The forest and the mountain were moving at great speed over the sea towards the shores of Ireland, and the swineherds ran back to the king's hall to tell what they had seen.

Matholwch, being only a man even if he was king, asked his wife for the answer to this mystery. Branwen wiped the grease from her hands and the sweat from her eyes and smiled. 'Your pig-men have seen the army of the Island of the Mighty, the warriors of Britain, and the forest is the masts of their ships. And they have also seen a mountain, which is my brother Bran, and the high ridge upon the mountain is his nose, and the two lakes are his two eyes watering with rage at the insult you have laid upon me.'

The warriors of Ireland ran in fear over the River Shannon, and broke the bridge behind them, trusting to the power of a sacred stone within the waters to protect them. But when Bran followed them he stretched out and bridged the river with his body, for he who would be a chieftain must first be a bridge. Thus the Britons and their allies crossed to the other side. Matholwch was so terrified that he sent messengers seeking peace, and offered the throne of Ireland to Gwern, son of Branwen and sister-son of Bran, for in that land the power descended through the female line. But Bran resolved to rule Ireland himself, and to have the satisfaction of getting it from Matholwch.

The Irish druids suggested that a great house be built for Bran, the first that was big enough to hold him, and that the kingdom of Ireland would be bestowed upon him by ceremony in this house. But the house was a trick to defeat Bran by treachery, for none could defeat him in open battle. The great house had one hundred pillars supporting its high roof, and upon every pillar hung a leather bag, and in each bag an armed warrior was hiding, ready to slash his way out and kill Bran.

Evnissyen, the bringer of strife and change, looked at the hundred bags and asked an Irishman what was in them. 'Oatmeal for making the celebration porridge,' was the reply, so Evnissyen, suspecting a trick, squeezed each bag between his strong hands until all hundred warriors were squeezed to death.

When the Irish and the Britons met in the great house, it was resolved that all should acknowledge Bran as overlord and do homage to him, but that Gwern, son of Branwen, sister-son of Bran, should be the new king of Ireland. After the rituals of kingship, Gwern went in turn to each of his uncles from the Island of the Mighty, to Bran the Blessed, to Manawyddan, to Nissyen, and they embraced him. But Evnissyen son of Penardun snatched the youth up into the air by his feet, and flung him headlong into the great sacred fire in the centre of the hall. Branwen was distraught with grief and tried to run into the flames after her son, but Bran caught her and held her fast.

So every Irish warrior and every warrior of the host of Bran snatched up weapons and began a terrible battle that lasted for many nights and days. The slaughter was appalling, and the Irish came to have the upper hand, for they flung their dead into the great cauldron that Bran had given to Matholwch and brought them back to life. When Evnissyen realized how the Irish were winning the conflict he resolved to put a stop to it, and, casting off his shoes, tearing his clothes to reveal his bare buttocks and smearing clay over his face, he disguised himself as an Irishman. When the Irish came seeking their dead to throw into the cauldron, Evnissyen lay upon the hard ground and played dead, but when they threw him in, he stretched and stretched until his heart burst and the cauldron shattered into four pieces.

Then the warriors of Britain killed the warriors of Ireland, but at the end of the battle there were only seven of Bran's great host left alive. These seven were Pryderi, Manawyddan, Gluneu son of Taran, the bard Taliesin, Ynawc, Grudyen son of Muryel, and Heilyn son of Gwynn the ancient. Bran was wounded in the foot by a poisoned dart, and knew that he had not long to live. So he gave these instructions and prophecies to his seven companions: 'Cut off my head, and carry it to the White Hill in London, and bury it there facing towards the shores of France. And you shall be a long time upon the road. In Harlech you will feast for seven years with the birds of Rhiannon singing to you, and in those years the head will be as good a companion to you as it was when it was on my body. Then you will be eighty years at Gwales in Penvro [Gresham island, off the Pembroke coast] and the head will be with you uncorrupted until someone opens the door that looks towards Aber Henvelen and towards Cornwall. And after that door has been opened you must go straight to London and bury the head to guard the Island of the Mighty.'

The seven companions, with Branwen as the eighth, cut off the head of Bran, sailed back to Wales, and made land at Aber Alaw, a river in the island of Anglesey. Branwen looked first towards Ireland, then towards Britain, and said, 'Alas that two islands have been destroyed because of me,' and her heart broke, and she died. The seven companions made her a four-sided grave by the River Alaw, and today this is the mound called Ynys Branwen.

As they journeyed towards Harlech with the severed head, they met a great number of men and women on the road, and asked them for news of what had happened in the kingdom while they were away in Ireland.

'Have you any tidings?' asked Manawyddan.

'We have none,' they replied, 'only that Caswallawn the son of Beli has conquered the Island of the Mighty and is crowned king in London.'

'What has become of Caradawc, son of Bran, and the seven who were left with him to rule the Britons?' asked Manawyddan.

'Caswallawn came upon them and slew six of them and Caradawc died of grief when his heart broke, for he could see the sword that slew the men, but could not see the slayer. Caswallawn had the Veil of Illusion upon himself, so no one could see him slay the six men, but he could not bring himself to kill Caradawc, because he was his nephew, the son of his cousin. Only Pendaran Dyved, a page with those men, escaped into the wood.'

And so three died of broken hearts: Evnissyen, Branwen and Caradawc.

The company arrived at Harlech as Bran had foretold, and they feasted there for seven years with the three birds of Rhiannon singing to them. So beautiful was the song of these birds that all the songs that the seven had heard before seemed ugly, and the birds seemed to be at a great distance from them over the sea, yet they were as clear and distinct as if they were close by. When the seventh year had ended they travelled to Gwales in Penvro, where there was a fair location overlooking the sea, and a great hall with two doors open, but the third door facing towards Cornwall was shut tight.

They remained in that place for eighty years, not knowing how long had passed, and forgetting all joys and sorrows in the company of the head of Bran, which conversed with them as they ate and drank. And this time out of time was called the Entertaining of the Noble Head, whereas the Entertaining of Branwen and Matholwch was during their time in Ireland.

Celtic brooch: a classic example of Celtic jewellery.

One day Heilyn son of Gwynn awoke from out of his happy dream, and became determined to see what lay beyond the third door. So he opened the door and looked towards Aber Henvelen and on to Cornwall. And once the door was opened, they all looked through it, just as Bran had prophesied. With one glance they were suddenly aware, and remembered all the evils they had suffered, all the friends they had lost, all the misery that had come upon them. They were so troubled by their sorrow that they knew no rest, but set out upon the long road to London with the sacred head of Bran.

The companions buried the head within the White Mount, as they had been bidden. This was the third good concealment of which the bards tell, and when the head was dug up again it was the third unlucky disclosure, for the buried head had guarded against invasion from the lands across the sea to the east.

In Ireland there were only five pregnant women left alive, living in a cave in the wilderness. In one night these five women gave birth to five sons, and they nursed these sons until they grew to manhood. Then each of the five young men took the mother of one of his companions as a wife, and so they repopulated the country, seeking out gold and silver from the great battle fields and becoming wealthy. And it is from these original five that the land of Ireland has its five zones or counties today.

Here ends this branch of the Mabinogi, which tells of the third unhappy blow of the Island, which was given to Branwen, and which tells of the convocation of Bran when the armies of one hundred and fifty lands went over to Ireland to avenge that blow, and of the great feast in Harlech and the singing birds of Rhiannon, and the celebration of the severed head for eighty years.

2

the Wooing
of Etain
(ireland)

This myth is found in various forms worldwide, and has many levels of meaning. It tells of love and the human soul, of the spirit coming into birth, and of the madness and divine potential of love between mortal and fairy beings. Like many Celtic legends, it involves the qualities and powers of kingship, which is conferred by otherworldly powers, by the Goddess of the Land.

One of the best modern renderings of the story is *The Immortal Hour*, a drama written by William Sharp under his famous pen-name Fiona Macleod. This was set to music by Rutland Boughton in the early twentieth century, to create the immensely popular Celtic opera of the same name. In that interpretation the tragic theme of lost love and longing for the fairy realm is paramount. In this version, translated in the nineteenth century from original sources and reprinted here from *Ancient Irish Tales*, edited by T. P. Cross and C. H. Slover, 1936, it is the battle between mortal and fairy kings for the empowering Etain, who is at once lover and goddess, immensely powerful yet mysterious and inscrutable.

*T*HERE was an admirable, noble king in the high-kingship over Ireland; namely, Eochaid Airem . . . The first year after he ascended the throne, a proclamation was made throughout Ireland that the feast of Tara was to be celebrated, and that all the men of Ireland should attend it, that their taxes and their levies might be known. And the one answer made by all the men of Ireland to Eochaid's summons was that they would not attend the feast of Tara during such time, whether it be long or short, as the king of Ireland was without a wife that was suitable for him; for there was not a noble of the men of Ireland who was without a wife suitable for him, and there was not a king without a queen, and there would not come a man without his wife to the feast of Tara, nor would there come a woman without a husband.

Thereupon Eochaid sent out from him his horsemen, and his entertainers, and his spies, and his messengers of the border throughout Ireland, and they searched all Ireland for a woman who should be suitable for the king in respect to form and grace and countenance and birth. And besides all this, there was one more condition regarding her: the king would never take a wife who had been given to any one else before him. And the king's officers sought all Ireland, both south and north, and they found at Inber Cichmany a woman suitable for him: that is, Etain the daughter of Etar, who was king of Echrad. Then his messengers returned to Eochaid and gave him a description of the maiden in regard to form and grace and countenance.

And Eochaid set forth to take the maiden, and the way that he went was across the fair green of Bri Leith. And there he saw a maiden upon the brink of a spring. She held in her hand a comb of silver decorated with gold. Beside her, as for washing, was a basin of silver whereon was chased four golden birds, and there were little bright gems of carbuncle set in the rim of the basin. A cloak pure purple, hanging in folds about her, and beneath it a mantle with silver borders, and a brooch of gold in the garment over her bosom. A tunic with a long hood about her, and as for it, smooth and glossy. It was made of greenish silk behind red

Doorway to round tower, Donaghmore, Ireland.

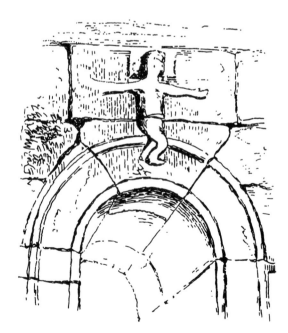

embroidery of gold, and marvellous bow-pins of silver and gold upon her breasts in the tunic, so that the redness of the gold against the sun in the green silk was clearly visible to the men. Two tresses of golden hair upon her head, and a plaiting of four strands in each tress, and a ball of gold upon the end of each plait.

And the maiden was there loosening her hair to wash it, and her two arms out through the armholes of her smock. As white as the snow of one night was each of her two arms, and as red as the foxglove of the mountain was each of her two cheeks. As blue as the hyacinth was each of her two eyes; delicately red her lips; very high, soft and white her two shoulders. Tender, smooth and white were her two wrists; her fingers long and very white; her nails pink and beautiful. As white as snow or as the foam of the wave was her side, slender, long and as soft as silk. Soft, smooth and white were her thighs; round and small, firm and white were her two knees; as straight as a rule were her two ankles; slim and foam-white were her two feet. Fair and very beautiful were her two eyes; her eyebrows blackish blue like the shell of a beetle. It was she the maiden who was the fairest and the most beautiful that the eyes of men had ever seen; and it seemed probable to the king and his companions that she was out of a fairy mound. This is the maiden concerning whom is spoken the proverb: 'Every lovely form must be tested by Etain, every beauty by the standard of Etain.'

A desire for her seized the king immediately, and he sent a man of his company to hold her before him. Then Eochaid approached the maiden and questioned her. 'Whence art thou, o maiden?' said the king, 'and whence hast thou come?'

'Not hard to answer,' replied the maiden. 'Etain the daughter of the king of Echrad out of the fairy-mounds I am called.'

'Shall I have an hour of dalliance with thee?' said Eochaid.

'It is for that I have come hither under thy protection,' said she. 'I have been here for twenty years since I was born in the fairy-mound, and the men of the fairy-mound, both kings and nobles, have been wooing me, and naught was got by any of them from me, because I have loved thee and given love and affection to thee since I was a little child and since I was capable of speaking. It was for the noble tales about thee and for thy splendour that I have loved thee, and, although I have never seen thee before, I recognized thee at once by thy description. It is thou, I know, to whom I have attained,' said she.

'That is by no means the invitation of a bad friend,' replied Eochaid. ' Thou shalt be welcomed by me, and all other women shall be left for thy sake, and with thee alone will I live as long as it is pleasing to thee.'

'Give me my fitting bride-price,' said the maiden, 'and thereafter let my desire be fulfilled.'

'That shall be to thee,' said the king.

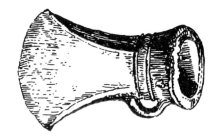

The value of seven bond-slaves was given to her for a bride-price, and after that he took her with him to Tara, and a truly hearty welcome was given to her.

Now there were three brothers of one blood who were the sons of Finn: Eochaid Airem and Eochaid Fedlech and Ailill Anglonnach, or Ailill of the One Stain, because the only stain that was upon him was that he loved his brother's wife. At that time came the men of Ireland to hold the feast of Tara, and they were there fourteen days before Samain and fourteen days after Samain. It was at the feast of Tara that Ailill Anglonnach fell in love with Etain the daughter of Etar. Ailill gazed at the woman as long as he was at the feast of Tara. Then Ailill's wife, the daughter of Luchta Red-Hand from the borders of Leinster, said to her husband: 'Ailill,' said she, 'why doest thou keep gazing far off from thee? For such long-looking is a sign of love.' Thereupon Ailill became ashamed and blamed himself for that thing, and he did not look at Etain after that.

After the feast of Tara the men of Ireland separated from one another, and then it was that the pains of jealousy and great envy filled Ailill, and a heavy illness came upon him. As a result he was carried to Dun Fremain in Tethba, the favourite stronghold of his brother, the king. Ailill remained there to the end of a year in long-sickness and in long-pining, but he did not confess the cause of his sickness to any one. And thither came Eochaid to enquire after Ailill. He put his hand upon Ailill's breast, whereupon Ailill heaved a sigh.

'Now,' said Eochaid, 'the sickness in which thou art does not appear to be serious. How is everything with thee?'

'By my word,' replied Ailill, 'not easier is it with me, but worse in all respects every day and every night.'

'What ails thee?' asked Eochaid.

'By my true word,' said Ailill, 'I do not know.'

'Let there be brought to me someone who shall make known the cause of this illness,' said Eochaid.

Then was brought to them Fachtna, the physician of Eochaid. And Fachtna put his hand upon Ailill's breast, and Ailill sighed.

'Now,' said Fachtna, 'the matter is not serious. There is nothing the matter with thee but one of two things; that is, either the pains of jealousy or love which thou hast given, and thou hast found no help till now.' Thereupon Ailill was ashamed. He did not confess the cause of his illness to the physician, and the physician went from him.

Now, as regards Eochaid, he went out to make his royal circuit throughout Ireland, and he left Etain in the stronghold of Fremain, and he said to her: 'Deal gently with Ailill as long as he is alive, and should he die,' said he, 'have his grave of sod dug, and let his pillar-stone be raised, and let his name be written on it in ogham.' The king then departed on his royal circuit of Ireland, leaving Ailill there in Dun Fremain in expectation of death and dissolution for the space of that year.

Into the house in which Ailill was, Etain used to go each day to consult with and minister to him. One day she asked him: 'What is the matter with thee? Thy sickness is indeed great, and if we knew anything that would satisfy thee, thou shouldst get it from us.' It was thus that she spoke, and she sang a little lay and Ailill answered her . . .

Etain continued to come every day to Ailill to bathe him and to divide his food for him, and she helped him greatly, for she was sad at seeing him perish because of her. One day she said to Ailill, 'Come tomorrow at daybreak to tryst with me in the house that stands outside the stronghold, and there shalt thou have granted thy request and thy desire.' On that night Ailill lay without sleep until the coming of the morning; and when the time had come that was appointed for his tryst, his sleep lay heavily upon him; so that till the hour of his rising he lay deep in his sleep. And Etain went to the tryst, nor had she long to wait ere she saw a man coming towards her in the likeness of Ailill, weary and feeble; but she knew that he was not Ailill, and continued there waiting for Ailill.

Wrist torque or serpent bracelet.

And the lady came back from her tryst, and Ailill awoke, and thought that he would rather die than live; and he was in great sadness and grief. And the lady came to speak with him, and when he told her what had befallen him: 'Come,' said she, 'to the same place to meet with me tomorrow.' And upon the morrow it was the same as upon the first day; each day came the same man to her tryst. And she came again upon the last day that was appointed for the tryst, and the same man met her. ''Tis not with thee that I trysted,' said she, 'why dost thou come to meet me? And for him whom I would have met here, neither from desire of his love nor for fear of harm from him had I appointed to meet him, but only to heal him, and to cure him from the sickness which had come upon him for his love of me.'

'It were more fitting for thee to come to tryst with me,' said the man, 'for when thou wast Etain, daughter of the king of Echrad, and when thou wast the daughter of Ailill, I myself was thy first husband.'

'Why,' said she, 'what is thy name at all, if it were to be demanded of thee?'

'It is not hard to answer thee,' he said. 'Mider of Bri Leith is my name.'

'And what made thee to part from me, if we were as thou sayest?' said Etain.

'Easy again is the answer,' said Mider. 'It was the sorcery of Fuamnach and the spells of Bressal Etarlam that put us apart.' And Mider said to Etain: 'Wilt thou come with me?'

'Nay,' answered Etain, 'I will not exchange the king of all Ireland for thee; for a man whose kindred and whose lineage is unknown.'

'It was I myself indeed,' said Mider, ' who filled all the mind of Ailill with love for thee; it was I also who prevented his coming to the tryst with thee, and allowed him not to spoil thy honour.'

After all this the lady went back to her house, and she came to speech with Ailill, and she greeted him. 'It hath happened well for us both,' said Ailill, 'that the man met thee there, for I am cured for ever from my illness, thou art also unhurt in thine honour, and may a blessing rest upon thee!'

'Thanks be to our gods,' said Etain, 'that both of us do indeed deem that all this hath chanced so well.'

And after that, Eochaid came back from his royal progress, and he asked at once for his brother; and the tale was told to him from the beginning to the end, and the king was grateful to Etain, in that she had been gracious to Ailill. 'What hath been related in this tale,' said Eochaid, 'is well pleasing to ourselves.'

Now upon another time it chanced that Eochaid Airem, the king of Tara, arose upon a certain fair day in the time of summer and he ascended the high ground of Tara to behold the plain of Breg; beautiful was the colour of that plain, and there was upon it excellent blossom, glowing with all hues that are known. And, as the aforesaid Eochaid looked about and around him, he saw a young strange warrior upon the high ground at his side. The tunic that the warrior wore was purple in colour, his hair was of golden yellow, and of such length that it reached to the edge of his shoulders. The eyes of the young warrior were lustrous and grey; in the one hand he held a five-pointed spear, in the other a shield with a white central boss, and with gems of gold upon it. And Eochaid held his peace, for he knew that none such had been in Tara on the night before, and the gate that led into the enclosure had not at that hour been thrown open.

The warrior came, and placed himself under the protection of Eochaid.

'Welcome do I give,' said Eochaid, 'to the hero who is yet unknown.'

'Thy reception is such as I expected when I came,' said the warrior.

'We know thee not,' answered Eochaid.

'Yet thee in truth I know well!' he replied.

'What is the name by which thou art called?' said Eochaid.

'My name is not known to renown,' said the warrior. 'I am Mider of Bri Leith.'

'And for what purpose art thou come?' said Eochaid.

'I have come that I may play a game of chess with thee,' answered Mider.

'Truly,' said Eochaid, 'I myself am skilful at chess-play.'

'Let us test that skill!' said Mider.

'Nay,' said Eochaid, 'the queen is even now in her sleep, and hers is the apartment in which the chessboard lies.'

'I have here with me,' said Mider, ' a chessboard which is not inferior to thine.' It was even as he said, for that chessboard was silver, and the men to play with were gold; and upon that board were costly stones, casting their light on every side, and the bag that held the men was of woven chains of brass.

Mider then set out the chessboard, and he called upon Eochaid to play. 'I will not play,' said Eochaid, 'unless we play for a stake.'

'What stake shall we have upon the game then?' said Mider.

'It is indifferent to me,' said Eochaid.

'Then,' said Mider, 'if thou dost obtain the forfeit of my stake, I will bestow on thee fifty steeds of a dark grey, their heads of a blood-red colour, but dappled; their ears pricked high, and their chests broad; their nostrils wide, and their hoofs slender; great is their strength, and they are keen like a whetted edge; eager are they, high-standing and spirited, yet easily stopped in their course.'

Several games were played between Eochaid and Mider, and since Mider did not put forth his whole strength, the victory on all occasions

Knotted torque of gold (pre-Celtic).

rested with Eochaid. But instead of the gifts which Mider had offered, Eochaid demanded that Mider and his folk should perform for him services which should be of benefit to his realm: that he should clear away the rocks and stones from the plains of Meath, should remove the rushes which made the land barren around his favourite fort of Tethba, should cut down the forest of Breg, and finally should build a causeway across the moor or bog of Lamrach that men might pass freely across it.

All these things Mider agreed to do, and Eochaid sent his steward to see how that work was done. And when it came to the time after sunset, the steward looked, and he saw that Mider and his fairy host, together with fairy oxen, were labouring at the causeway over the bog; and thereupon much of earth and of gravel and of stones was poured into it. Now it had, before that time, always been the custom of the men of Ireland to harness their oxen with a strap over their foreheads, so that the pull might be against the foreheads of the oxen; and this custom lasted up to that very night, when it was seen that the fairy folk had placed the yoke upon the shoulders of the oxen so that the pull might be there; and in this way were the yokes of the oxen afterwards placed by Eochaid, and thence comes the name by which he is known: even Eochaid Airem, or Eochaid the Ploughman, for he was the first of all the men of Ireland to put the yokes on the necks of the oxen, and thus it became the custom for all the land of Ireland. And this is the song that the host of the fairies sang, as they laboured at the making of the road:

Thrust it in hand! force it in hand!
Noble this night, the troop of oxen:
Hard is the task that is asked, and who
From the bridging of Lamrach shall receive gain or harm?

Not in all the world could a road have been found that should be better than the road that they made, had it not been that the fairy folk were observed as they worked upon it; but for that cause a breach has been made in that causeway. And the steward of Eochaid thereafter came to him; and he described to him that great labouring band that had come before his eyes, and he said that there was not over the chariot-pole of life a power that could withstand its might. And, as they spoke thus with each other, they saw Mider standing before them; high was he girt, and ill-favoured was the face that he showed; and Eochaid arose, and he gave welcome to him.

'Thy welcome is such as I expected when I came,' said Mider. 'Cruel and senseless hast thou been in thy treatment of me, and much of hardship and suffering hast thou given me. All things that seemed good in thy sight have I got for thee, but now anger against thee hath filled my mind!'

'I return not anger for anger,' answered Eochaid. 'What thou wishest shall be done.'

'Let it be as thou wishest,' said Mider. 'Shall we play at the chess?' said he.

'What stake shall we set upon the game?' said Eochaid.

'Even such stake as the winner of it shall demand,' said Mider. And in that very place Eochaid was defeated, and he forfeited his stake.

'My stake is forfeited to thee,' said Eochaid.

'Had I wished it, it had been forfeited long ago,' said Mider.

'What is it that thou desirest me to grant?' said Eochaid.

'That I may hold Etain in my arms and obtain a kiss from her!' answered Mider.

Eochaid was silent for a while, and then he said: 'One month from this day thou shalt come, and that very thing that thou hast asked for shall be given to thee.'

Now for a year before that Mider first came to Eochaid for the chess-play, had he been at the wooing of Etain, and he obtained her not; and the name which he gave to Etain was Befind, or Fair-haired Woman, so it was that he said:

Wilt thou come with me, fair-haired woman?

as has before been recited. And it was at that time that Etain said: 'If thou obtainest me from him who is the master of my house, I will go; but if thou art not able to obtain me from him, then I will not go.' And thereupon Mider came to Eochaid, and allowed him at the first to win the victory over him, in order that Eochaid should stand in his debt; and therefore it was that he paid the great stakes to which he had agreed, and therefore also was it that he had demanded of him that he should play that game in ignorance of what was staked. And when Mider and his

folk were paying those agreed-on stakes, which were paid upon th
night; to wit, the making of the road, and the clearing of the stones frc
Meath, the rushes from around Tethba, and the forest that is over Bre
it is thus that he spoke, as it is written in the *Book of Drum Snechta:*

> Pile on the soil; thrust on the soil;
> Red are the oxen who labour;
> Heavy the troops that obey my words.
> Heavy they seem, and yet men are they.
> Strongly, as piles, are the tree-trunks placed:
> Red are the wattles bound above them:
> Tired are your hands, and your glances slant;
> One woman's winning this toil may yield!
> Oxen ye are, but revenge shall see;
> Men who are white shall be your servants;
> Rushes from Tethba are cleared:
> Grief is the price that the man shall pay:
> Stones have been cleared from the rough Meath ground;
> Whose shall the gain or the harm be?

Now Mider appointed a day at the end of the month when he was
meet Eochaid, and Eochaid called the armies of the heroes of Irela
together, so that they came to Tara; and all the best of the champions
Ireland, ring within ring, were about Tara, and they were in the midst
Tara itself, and they guarded it, both without and within; and the ki
and the queen were in the midst of the palace, and the outer court there
was shut and locked, for they knew that the great might of men wou
come upon them. And upon the appointed night Etain was dispensi
the banquet to the kings, for it was her duty to pour out the wine, wh
in the midst of their talk they saw Mider standing before them in t
centre of the palace. He was always fair, yet fairer than he ever w
seemed Mider to be upon that night. And he brought to amazement
the hosts on which he gazed, and all thereupon were silent, and the kir
gave a welcome to him.

'Thy reception is such as I expected when I came,' said Mider. 'I
that now be given to me that has been promised. 'Tis a debt that is d
when a promise hath been made, and I for my part have given to thee
that was promised by me.'

'I have not yet considered the matter,' said Eochaid.

'Thou hast promised Etain's very self to me,' said Mider. 'That is wl
has come from thee.'

Etain blushed for shame when she heard that word.

'Blush not,' said Mider to Etain, 'for in no wise has thy wedding-fe
been disgraced. I have been seeking thee for a year with the fairest jew
and treasures that can be found in Ireland, and I have not taken thee ur

the time came when Eochaid might permit it. 'Tis not through any will of thine that I have won thee.'

'I myself told thee,' said Etain, 'that until Eochaid should resign me to thee I would grant thee nothing. Take me then for my part, if Eochaid is willing to resign me to thee.'

'But I will not resign thee!' said Eochaid. 'Nevertheless, he shall take thee in his arms upon the floor of this house as thou art.'

'It shall be done!' said Mider.

He took his weapons in his left hand and the woman beneath his right shoulder; and he carried her off through the smoke-hole of the house. And the hosts rose up around the king, for they felt that they had been disgraced, and they saw two swans circling round Tara, and the way that they took was the way to the elf-mound of Femen. And Eochaid with an army of the men of Ireland went to the elf-mound of Femen, which men call the mound of the Fair-haired Woman. And he followed the counsel of the men of Ireland, and he dug up each of the elf-mounds that he might take his wife from thence. And Mider and his host opposed them and the war between them was long: again and again the trenches made by Eochaid were destroyed; for nine years, as some say, lasted the strife of the men of Ireland to enter into the fairy place. And when at last the armies of Eochaid came by digging to the borders of the fairy-mound of Bri Leith, Mider sent to the side of the palace sixty women all in the shape of Etain, and so like to her that none could tell which was the queen, and Eochaid himself was deceived, and he chose instead of Etain her daughter Mess Buachalla (or, as some say, Esa). But when he found that he had been deceived, he returned again to sack Bri Leith, and this time Etain made herself known to Eochaid by proofs that he could not mistake, and he bore her away in triumph to Tara, and there she abode with the king.

3   the Curse of Macha
(Ireland)

Macha is a horse goddess, though she is disguised in this legend as a woman who races against horses. Horse goddesses, such as Epona of the Gauls or Rhiannon of the Welsh (and the princess-horse who helps N'oun-Doaré in the next chapter), were powerful deities in pagan Celtic religion.

Emain Macha is an ancient site (now called Navan Fort) near Armagh (Ard Macha) in Ulster. It is associated with the goddess or sacred queen Macha at the primal levels of its myth and folklore, and with the Ulster Red Branch warriors, and the hero Cuchulainn (see Chapters 5 and 10). One of the most curious aspects of the site is that close to the remains of a royal dwelling is a ritual building, a circular hall of massive size, that was built then deliberately burnt down without any apparent 'use'. The short poem after the story was inspired by a visit to Navan Fort in 1991.

CRUNNIUC son of Agnoman of the Ulaid was a noble with great lands and holdings. He lived in the wild places in the remote mountains with his sons, for his wife was long dead. One day, when he was alone in his hall, he saw a beautiful woman coming to him. She simply moved in and set about women's tasks, just as if she had always been there. And at night, she slept with Crunniuc. She was with him for a long time and brought him great luck and prosperity, and he and his people did not want for food or clothing, gifts to give, or fine jewels.

One day the Ulaid held a gathering for trade and business, and recreation and pleasure, and deals and bartering, and gifts and music and story-telling. Everyone travelled to it, the men and women, sons and daughters, slaves and free, oathbound and lovebound. Crunniuc set out with a will, wearing his best clothes and with a shining ruddy face.

'Take care to say nothing foolish,' she cautioned him.

'Not me, I shall keep myself to myself and you can be sure I will not be foolish or boastful,' he replied.

The great gathering was held, and so many men were sick with drinking and eating that it was deemed a huge success. At the end of the day the king's chariot was brought on to the field to race against all-comers and this royal chariot and horses were utterly victorious, even when the competitors dared to run their fastest. The assembled warriors said, 'Nothing is as fast as those horses.' But Crunniuc, who had been drinking with his cousins and driving bargains for exchanges of goods and slaves, said, 'My wife is as fast, and even faster.'

He was taken to the king at once to repeat his boastful challenge, and word was carried to his wife.

'A great misfortune has come to me,' she lamented, 'having to go and free this drunken boaster when I am about to give birth to his child.'

'Misfortune or not to you,' said the messenger, 'the man will die if you do not come and race against the king's horses, for he has sworn that you are as fast as they, and even faster.'

She went to the gathering and labour pains seized her. 'Help me,' she said to the assembled warriors, 'for a mother bore every one of you. Let the race wait until my children are born.' She failed to move them, and it was time for her to run. 'Well then,' she cried at the top of her voice, 'the evil you suffer will be greater than my pains, and it will afflict the Ulaid for a long time.'

'What is your name?' asked the king.

'My name and that of my children will mark this assembly place for ever. I am Macha daughter of Sainrith son of Imbath,' she said.

Bronze trumpet.

The Glenlyon Brooch, with motif of the Four Directions.

She raced against the chariot, and as it reached the end of the course marked out she had a son and a daughter. That is why the place is called Emain Macha.

At her delivery, she swore that any man who heard her screaming would himself suffer the pangs of birth for five days and four nights. All the Ulaid who were there were afflicted by the curse, and also their descendants suffered from it for nine generations afterwards. Five days and four nights was the extent of the labour pains of the Ulaid, and for nine generations the Ulaid were repeatedly as weak as a woman in labour. Three groups of people only did not suffer from the curse. These were the women and the boy and girl children of Cuchulainn. Such was the cursed inheritance of the Ulaid from the time of Crunniuc son of Agnoman son of Curir Ulad son of Fiatach son of Urmi until the time of Furcc son of Dallan son of Manech son of Lugaid.

And to this day you can travel to Emain Macha, and see the great works of the ancestors there, where she drew out a circle with her brooch for the ground plan of her palace when she became queen, and where the warriors still sleep beneath the green earth, waiting to return. But that is another story.

Neck torque: the emblem of royalty and divinity.

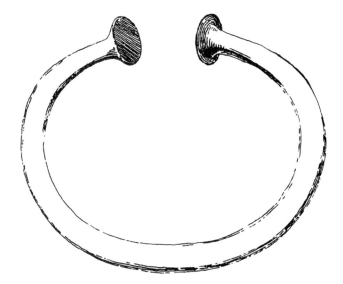

Macha

In Navan Fort I sought Cuchulainn,
Hero, spear, and sword-hung warrior,
But found Macha, noble queen,
With memories of palace, lake, and court.

Her tall nobles rapt in green turf
Plunge in deep sleep, long sleep,
'Wake us not,' they murmur, barely turning,
'We rest.'

Macha removed herself from Armagh,
From her old fortress on the hilltop,
Two thousand years before the Christians took it,
Plugged it with a church,
Clamped tight with retribution.

Macha in her fine new hall at Navan,
With her sacred horses and her Barbary ape,
Made offerings in the sacred lake,
Dug deep, filled high.

And on certain mornings when a queen might look
Both backwards and forwards in one hard stare,
Turned towards her old hilltop rath,
Where one day Christians would come.

At the last, the closing
Of her lovely palace,
High hall, brooch-encircle, sacred lake,
The people, Macha's children,
Raised a great wooden temple
Where the royal house had been.
They filled its sacred space with stones
And fired it.

Over the ashes of wood upon stone
Was earth cast,
In the perfect way, the mantle of peace.
The mound was never used again.

R. J. Stewart, 12 March 1991

4 'í don't know': the tale of n'oun-doaré (brittany)

The Celtic traditions of Brittany are in some ways more complex and yet in others more primitive than those of Wales, Ireland or Scotland. By primitive I mean earlier or foundational, and no value judgement is intended. This particular legend is a perfect demonstration of the rich Breton tradition that exists in oral tales. It is an initiatory or shamanistic tale, involving animal and spirit allies who come to the aid of a naïve young man bent upon a seemingly impossible quest.

ONE day, when the Marquis of Coat-Squiriou was returning from Morlaix, accompanied by his servant, he saw a four-or five-year-old boy lying asleep in the ditch. He dismounted, woke up the boy and said, 'What are you doing there, little one?'

'I don't know,' replied the boy.

'Who is your father?'

'I don't know.'

'And your mother?'

'I don't know.'

'Where do you come from?'

'I don't know.'

'What's your name?'

'I don't know' was all the boy could answer.

The Marquis told his servant to take him up on his horse and they went on their way home to Coat-Squiriou.

The boy was named N'oun-Doaré, which means 'I don't know' in Breton. They sent him to school at Carhaix, and he was a good scholar there, learning everything that he was taught.

Some years passed, and when N'oun-Doaré was twenty the Marquis said to him, 'Now you are educated enough, you should come home with me to Coat-Squiriou,' and this he did. On the 14th of October the Marquis and N'oun-Doaré went together to the big fair at Morlaix and they stayed at the best inn.

'I am pleased with you,' said the Marquis to the young man, so they went together to an armourer and they looked at many good swords. None of them pleased the youth, so they left without having bought anything. While they were passing a scrap-metal-dealer's shop N'oun-Doaré stopped, saw an old rusty sword, seized it and exclaimed, 'This is the sword for me!'

'What! Look what a state it's in!' said the Marquis. 'It's good for nothing.'

'Buy it for me just as it is, please, and you'll see later that it's good for something,' said N'oun-Doaré. So the Marquis paid for the rusty old sword. It did not cost him very much and N'oun-Doaré took it, very happy with his gift, and so they went back together to Coat-Squiriou. The next day, N'oun-Doaré was looking at the old battered sword, when he saw some faint lettering under the rust, which he deciphered. It read: 'I am invincible.' 'Formidable!' said N'oun-Doaré to himself.

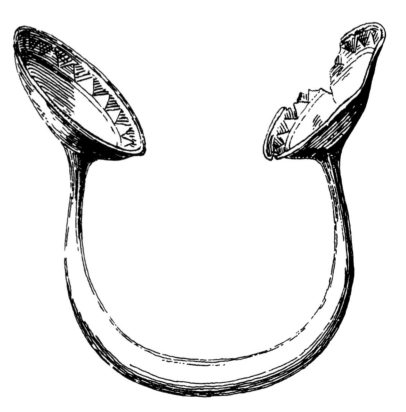

Gold ring with flower-calyx terminals.

Some time later the Marquis said to him, 'I think I should buy you a horse,' and they went together to Morlaix on fair day. So there they were, together, at the fairground. And certainly there were fine horses from Leon, Treguier and Cornwall. Yet N'oun-Doaré didn't find one to suit him, so by that evening after sunset, they left the fairground without having bought anything. On their way back, along St Nicholas Way, they met a Cornishman leading a worn-out old mare by a rope halter. It looked as thin as the Mare of Doom. N'oun-Doaré looked at the poor mare and said, 'That's the one for me.'

'What! That sorry nag? But just look at her!' said the Marquis.

'Yes, she's the one I want, and no other. Buy her for me, please.'

And the Marquis bought the old mare for N'oun-Doaré, wondering at his strange choice.

While handing over the mare, the Cornishman whispered in N'oun-Doare's ear, 'See these knots on the mare's halter?'

'Yes,' said N'oun-Doaré.

'Well, each time you untie one, the mare will immediately transport you fifteen hundred leagues from wherever you are.'

'Formidable!' said N'oun-Doaré. Then he and the Marquis went on their way back to Coat-Squiriou with the old mare.

As soon as he was there N'oun-Doaré undid a knot on the halter and the mare transported him instantly through the air, straight to the centre of Paris. Some months after this wonderful flight, the Marquis of Coat-Squiriou also came to Paris, and met N'oun-Doaré by chance in the street.

'What a surprise! Have you been here long?' he asked him.

'But of course,' said N'oun-Doaré.

'And did you get here?' asked the Marquis, so N'oun-Doaré told him how he had come to Paris.

The Marquis took him to greet the king in the royal palace. It happened that the king knew the Marquis well, and gave them a warm welcome.

One moonlit night, N'oun-Doaré went out alone on his skinny old mare, riding outside the city. He saw something shining at the foot of an old stone at the crossroads. As he came closer, he saw that it was a diamond-studded golden crown.

'I'll take that away in my coat,' he said aloud to himself.

'Take care, or you'll regret it,' said a mysterious voice from behind his ear. The voice was that of his mare, and she repeated this warning three times. N'oun-Doaré hesitated for a while, but eventually took the crown away, hidden under his coat.

The king had entrusted him to look after some of the royal horses, and at night he used the crown to light his stable, for the diamonds shone brightly in the darkness. N'oun-Doaré's horses were in better condition than those of the other grooms, and the king congratulated him. This made the others jealous. Of course, it was forbidden to have a light in the royal stables at night, and when they saw there was always one in N'oun-Doaré's stable the jealous grooms ran to tell the king.

At first, the king thought nothing of it, but when they repeated the accusation several times, he asked the Marquis of Coat-Squiriou if there was any truth in it.

'I don't know,' replied the Marquis, 'but I'll find out straight away from my servant.'

'The light comes from my rusty old sword,' said N'oun-Doaré, 'which shines in the darkness because it's a fairy sword.' He did not want anyone to know about the shining crown, and for a while they all believed him.

One night, however, his enemies peeped through the keyhole into the stable. They saw that the light came from a beautiful golden crown placed on the feed rack, and they saw that it shone without burning and was not consumed or diminished. So of course they ran and told the king. On the following night the king waited for the light from the crown to appear and suddenly burst into the stable. He went off with the crown hidden under his coat and took it straight to his private rooms.

The very next day the king called the wise men and magicians and astrologers to Paris, and demanded that they tell him how the crown shone and who was the true owner, but none of them could answer him, and they all made excuses. By chance there was a little child there who was just seven years old, and when he saw the crown he recognized it straight away and said it belonged to the Golden Ram Princess.

The king sent for N'oun-Doaré at once and spoke to him sternly. 'You must bring the Golden Ram Princess to my court to be my bride, and if you don't bring her to me it will be the death of you.'

Poor N'oun-Doaré was perplexed, and so he went to his old mare with tears in his eyes.

'I know what's upset you and made you sad,' said the old mare. 'Don't you remember I told you to leave that shining crown where you found it, otherwise you would regret it one day? Now that day has come. However, don't despair, for if you obey me and do exactly as I tell you, you will still get out of trouble. First, you must go to the king and ask him for oats and money for the journey.'

The king willingly gave both oats and money, and N'oun-Doaré set out, riding on his old mare. Eventually they came to the seashore and saw a little fish stranded on the sand, near to death.

'Put this little fish back in the sea quickly,' said the mare, and N'oun-Doaré hastened to obey.

Straight away the little fish lifted its head out of the water, and said, 'You have saved my life, N'oun-Doaré. I am the King of the Fish, and if you ever need my help, you have only to come to the seashore and call for me and I'll be with you at once.' The fish dived into the waves and disappeared.

So they travelled on, and soon they came across a little bird which had been trapped in a snare. 'Release this bird,' said the mare again. N'oun-Doaré released the little bird, which spoke aloud as it flew away. 'Thank

A cromlech, said to be the dwelling of ancestors and fairies in Celtic tradition in Ireland, Brittany and Scotland.

you, N'oun-Doaré, I'll return this favour. I am the King of the Birds and if ever I can be of service, you have only to call and I'll be with you at once.'

They continued on their way and the skinny old mare rapidly crossed the rivers, mountains, forests and sea. Soon they reached the high walls of the Golden Ram Castle, and a greater, more golden and shining castle had never been seen. They heard a terrifying sound coming from within the castle, so frightening that N'oun-Doaré dared not go in. By the door he saw a man chained to a tree. This man had as many horns on his body as there are days in the year.

'Unchain this man and set him free,' said the mare.

'I dare not go near him,' said N'oun-Doaré.

'Don't be afraid. He won't harm you.'

So, trembling with fear, N'oun-Doaré unchained the horned man, who said to him, 'Thank you, I'll return you this favour. If you ever need help, call for Griffescornu, King of the Underworld, and I'll come straight away.'

'Now go into the castle,' said the mare, 'and fear nothing. I'll stay here in the woods and you can find me when you come back out again. The Golden Ram Princess will welcome you warmly and show you all kinds of wonderful things. You must invite her to return to the woods with you to see me, your mare. Tell her that I am the best mare in the world, and that I know all the dances of Brittany, and those lesser dances found in other lands. Then you must tell her the mare will perform dances right before her very eyes, which is a wonder not to be missed.'

So N'oun-Doaré set off towards the castle door. Soon he met a servant who was getting water from the pure spring in the woods, who asked him what he was doing there.

'I wish to speak with the Golden Ram Princess,' he replied.

The servant ran and told his mistress that a stranger had just arrived at the castle to speak with her. The princess came straight down from her bedchamber and invited N'oun-Doaré to see all the wonders of the castle. When he had seen everything, so many wonders that they cannot be told here, it was his turn to invite the princess to come to the woods and see his magical dancing mare. She agreed straight away, as she had never seen a horse dance the dances of Brittany. The mare performed the most beautiful dances for her, which pleased her very much.

'Climb on her back, Princess,' said N'oun-Doaré softly, 'and she will happily dance with you.'

After only the briefest hesitation, the princess mounted the mare. N'oun-Doaré quickly jumped up behind her, and the mare rose up into the air and transported them in an instant, over and beyond the sea to Paris.

'You've tricked me!' shouted the princess, 'but you are not yet at the end of your trials and you'll weep more than once before I marry the old King of France.'

They went straight to Paris, and as soon as they were there N'oun-Doaré took the princess to the king, saying 'Your Majesty, here is the Golden Ram Princess.'

The king was overwhelmed by her beauty. He could not contain his happiness and wanted to marry her there and then. But the princess asked them first to bring her ring, which she had left in her bedchamber in the Golden Ram Castle. So the king charged N'oun-Doaré with the task of fetching the ring. In despair, N'oun-Doaré went back to his mare.

'Do you not remember,' said the mare, 'that you saved the life of the King of the Birds and that he promised to return the favour when the occasion arose?'

'I do indeed remember,' said N'oun-Doaré.

'Well, now's the time to call for his help.'

So N'oun-Doaré called out at the top of his voice, 'King of the Birds, King of the Birds, come and help me please!'

The King of the Birds came straight away and said, 'What can I do to help you, N'oun-Doaré?'

'The King of France,' he replied, 'commands me, under pain of death, to fetch him the ring which the Golden Ram Princess left locked in her castle, and for which she has lost the key.'

'Don't worry. The ring will be brought to you,' said the King of the Birds. And without delay he called every bird in the land, each by its own name.

They came as each of their names was called, but alas, not one of them was small enough to pass through the keyhole into the Golden Ram Castle. The very last bird to come was the wren, and she seemed small enough, so she was sent to try and fetch the ring. With great difficulty, and losing some feathers, she managed to squeeze through the keyhole, take the ring and bring it back to Paris. N'oun-Doare ran and gave it straight to the princess.

'Now, Princess,' said the king, 'surely you've no further need to delay my happiness?'

'I need only one more thing before I can satisfy you, Your Majesty,' she replied, 'but I need it badly, and there will be no wedding without it.'

'Speak, Princess,' said the king, 'and whatever you ask will be done.' And he said this knowing full well that he would demand not himself but N'oun-Doaré to do it, whatever it might be, on pain of death.

The princess smiled, drew a deep breath and said, 'Then have my castle brought here, facing yours.'

'Bring your castle here! How can you expect such a thing?'

'I must have my castle, I say to you, or there will be no wedding.'

And once more N'oun-Doaré was told to fulfil her wishes, and find a way of transporting the castle. With a heavy heart, he set out upon his skinny old mare.

When they arrived beneath the walls of the Golden Ram Castle the mare spoke behind his ear, saying, 'Ask the Horned King to help you, the one you released from his chains the first time you were here.'

So N'oun-Doaré called the King of the Underworld, who came instantly to his side and asked, 'How can I help you, N'oun-Doaré?'

'Transport the Golden Ram Castle to Paris, facing the king's palace, and do it right away,' gasped the young man.

'That's no problem. We'll do it in an instant.' The Horned King called his subjects from the realms below the land. A whole army of them came and they uprooted the castle from the rock on which it stood, took it up in the air and transported it swiftly to Paris. N'oun-Doaré and his mare followed them, and they all arrived at the same time.

In the morning the Parisians were astonished to see the sun rising and shining upon the golden domes of the magical castle. The light was so brilliant that they were sure there was a fire and they cried out from all sides, 'Fire, fire.' The princess recognized her own castle and ran to it.

'Now, Princess,' said the king, 'it only remains for you to name the wedding day.'

'Yes, but I need one more thing first', she said quickly, before the king could say another word.

'What is it, Princess?' he sighed.

'I must, of course, have the key to my castle. They haven't brought it to me, and I can't get in without it.'

'I have the best locksmiths in France at my command, and they'll make you a new one or die in the attempt!'

'No! No one in the world can make the key to open my castle door, and I must have the old one, which is at the bottom of the sea.' Then she explained that on her way to Paris, flying on the back of the old mare, she had dropped her key in the deepest part of the sea.

Once again N'oun-Doaré was told to satisfy her wishes, and to bring the princess the key to her castle. So he set off with his old mare. When they reached the seashore, he called for the King of the Fish, who came and said, 'What can I do for you, N'oun-Doaré?'

'I need the key to the Golden Ram Castle, which the princess has thrown into the sea.'

'Then you shall have it,' replied the King of the Fish, and at once he called all the fish of the sea, who rushed to him as he spoke their names, but none of them could find the key to the castle.

Now one fish came last to the call, and eventually he arrived with a priceless diamond in his mouth, complaining that it had slowed him down. And this, of course, was the key to the Golden Ram Castle. The

King of the Fish took it immediately and gave to N'oun-Doaré.

So N'oun-Doaré and his mare went swiftly back to Paris, happy and light-hearted this time, for they knew that their task was over.

The princess realized that she could no longer delay, and the day for the royal wedding was fixed. The court and the assembled nobility went to church with great pomp and ceremony, and everyone who was anyone was there to see the King of France wed the Golden Ram Princess.

N'oun-Doaré and his mare followed the procession and, to the astonishment and scandal of all present, they both went into the church, man and horse together, side by side. But when the wedding ceremony ended, the mare's skin fell off, revealing the most beautiful princess they had ever seen. She offered her hand to N'oun-Doaré, and said, 'I am the daughter of the King of Tartary. Come back with me to my own country and marry me, N'oun-Doaré.'

So, leaving the king and court dumbfounded, they vanished, and I've never heard of them since.

Standing stones: such pre-Celtic worship sites were the focus of many Celtic myths and legends.

5 the Wasting Sickness of Cuchulainn (Ireland)

This tale and 'The Wooing of Emer' (Chapter 10) are part of the vast saga or interlaced sequence involving Cuchulainn, the Ulster hero. On his mother's side, Cuchulainn was the grandson of the Daghda, whose name simply means 'The Good God'. The Daghda was a primal giant figure, one of the dimly remembered but extremely potent first deities of the Celts; many humorous and scurrilous tales were told about this lusty, powerful, hungry giant. As if this lineage was not sufficient, Cuchulainn was also said to be the son of Lugh Long-Hand, who name means 'Light', an image of the ancient Celtic sun god.

The mother of Cuchulainn was Dechtire, daughter of Maga, granddaughter of Angus 'Son of the Young', and half-sister to King Conchobar MacNessa. Thus the king and his champion or hero were related. As with the warriors of Arthur, or the ancient Greek heroes, we find echoes of divinity in legends concerning the origins of our hero; whoever or whatever Cuchulainn was originally, by the time the great tales and sagas had been built around his astonishing exploits and those of his men, he had assumed a magical and semi-divine nature.

In 'The Wasting Sickness' we have a classic story of the relationship between humans and fairy beings – a theme that occupies many Celtic myths and legends. Cuchulainn is scourged by two fairy maidens and remains in a trance in the human world for the duration of this contact. While he is thus weakened, the people of Ulster can be threatened by outside forces.

This version is reprinted from *Ancient Irish Tales*, edited by T. P. Cross and C. H. Slover, 1936.

EVERY year the men of Ulster were accustomed to hold festival together; and the time when they held it was for three days before Samain, and for three days after that day, and upon Samain itself. And the time that is spoken of is that when the men of Ulster used to assemble in Mag Muirthemne, and there they used to hold the festival every year; nor was there anything in the world that they would do at that time except sports, and marketings, and splendours, and pomps, and feasting and eating; and it is from that custom of theirs that the Festival of Samain was descended, that is now held throughout the whole of Ireland.

Now once upon a time the men of Ulster held festival in Mag Muirthemne, and the reason that this festival was held was that every man of them should every Samain give account of the combats he had made and of his valour.

It was their custom to hold that festival in order to give account of these combats, and the manner in which they gave that account was this: each man used to cut off the tip of the tongue of a foe whom he had killed, and carry it with him in a pouch. Moreover, in order to make more great the numbers of their contests, some used to bring with them the tips of the tongues of beasts, and each man publicly declared the fights he had fought, one man of them after the other. And they did this also: they laid their swords over their thighs when they related their combats, and their own swords used to turn against them when the strife that they declared was false; nor was this to be wondered at, for at that time it was customary for demons to scream from the weapons of men, so that for this cause their weapons might be the more able to guard them.

To that festival then came all the men of Ulster except two alone, and these two were Fergus mac Roig, and Conall the Victorious.

'Let the festival be held!' cried the men of Ulster.

'Nay,' said Cu Chulainn, 'it shall not be held until Conall and Fergus come,' and this he said because Fergus was the foster-father of Cu Chulainn, and Conall was his comrade.

Then said Sencha, 'Let us for the present engage in games of chess; and let the druids sing, and let the jugglers perform their feats.' And it was done as he had said.

Now while they were thus employed a flock of birds came down and hovered over a neighbouring lake; never were seen in Ireland more beautiful birds than these. And a longing that these birds should be given to them seized upon the women who were there, and each of them began to boast of the prowess of her husband at bird-catching.

'How I wish,' said Ethne, Conchobar's wife, 'that I could have two of those birds, one of them upon each of my two shoulders.'

'It is what we all long for,' said the women.

Two Romano-Celtic bronze pots, often said to be fairy kettles.

'If any should have this gift, I should be the first one to have it,' said the wife of Cu Chulainn.

'What are we to do now?' said the women.

'It is easy to answer you,' said Leborcham, the daughter of Oa and Adarc. 'I will go now with a message from you, and will seek for Cu Chulainn.'

She then went to Cu Chulainn. 'The women of Ulster would be well pleased,' she said, 'if yonder birds were given to them by thy hand.'

Cu Chulainn reached for his sword to unsheathe it against her. ' Cannot the women of Ulster find any other but us,' he said, 'to give them their bird-hunt today?'

'It is not seemly for thee to rage thus against them,' said Leborcham, 'for it is on thy account that the women of Ulster have assumed one of their three blemishes, even the blemish of blindness.' For there were three blemishes that the women of Ulster assumed, that of crookedness of gait, and that of a stammering in their speech, and that of blindness. Each of the women who loved Conall the Victorious had assumed a crookedness of gait; each woman who loved Cuscraid Menn, the Stammerer of Macha, Conchobar's son, stammered in her speech; each woman in like manner who loved Cu Chulainn had assumed a blindness of her eyes, in order to resemble Cu Chulainn; for he, when his mind was angry within him, was accustomed to draw in one of his eyes so far that a crane could not reach it in his head, and would thrust out the other so that it was as great as a cauldron in which a calf is cooked.

'Yoke for us the chariot, o Loeg!' said Cu Chulainn. At that Loeg yoked the chariot, and Cu Chulainn went into the chariot, and he cast his sword at the birds with a cast like the cast of a boomerang, so that they flapped against the water with their claws and wings. And they seized upon all the birds, and they gave them and distributed them among the women; nor was there any one of the women, except his wife alone, who had not a pair of those birds.

Then Cu Chulainn returned to his wife.

'Thou art angry,' said he to her.

'I am in no way angry,' she said, 'for I deem it as being by me that the distribution was made. And thou hast done what was fitting,' she said, 'for there is not one of those women but loves thee, none in whom thou hast no share; but for myself, none has any share in me but thou alone.'

'Be not angry,' said Cu Chulainn, 'if in the future any birds come to Mag Muirthemne or to the Boyne, the two birds that are the most beautiful among those that come shall be thine.'

A little while after this they saw two birds flying over the lake, linked together by a chain of red gold. They sang a gentle song, and a sleep fell upon all the men who were there except Cu Chulainn. Cu Chulainn rose up to pursue the birds.

'If thou wilt listen to me' said Loeg, 'thou wilt not go against them; behind those birds is some special power. Other birds may be taken by thee at some future day.'

'Is it possible that such claim as this should be made upon me?' said Cu Chulainn. 'Place a stone in my sling, o Loeg!'

Loeg thereon took a stone, and he placed it in the sling, and Cu Chulainn launched the stone at the birds, but the cast missed. 'Alas!' said he. He took another stone, and he launched this also at the birds, but the stone flew past them.

'Wretch that I am,' he cried, 'since the very first day that I assumed arms, I have never missed a cast until this day!' And he threw his spear at them, and the spear went through the shield of the wing of one of the birds, and the birds flew away, and went beneath the lake.

After this Cu Chulainn departed, and he rested his back against a stone pillar, and his soul was angry within him, and sleep fell upon him. Then saw he two women come to him: the one of them had a green mantle upon her, and upon the other was a purple mantle folded in five folds. And the woman in the green mantle approached him, and she laughed a laugh at him, and she gave him a stroke with a horsewhip. And then the other approached him, and she also laughed at him, and she struck him in the same way. For a long time were they thus, each of them in turn coming to him and striking him, until he was all but dead; and then they departed from him.

Now the men of Ulster perceived the state in which Cu Chulainn was, and they cried out that he should be awakened. But, 'Nay,' said Fergus, 'you shall not move him, for he is seeking a vision.' And a little after that Cu Chulainn arose from his sleep.

'What has happened to thee?' said the men of Ulster; but he had no power to bid greeting to them.

'Let me be carried,' he said, 'to the sick-bed that is in Tete Brece; not to Dun Imrith, nor yet to Dun Delgan.'

'Wilt thou not be carried to Dun Delgan, thy stronghold, to seek for Emer?' said Loeg.

'Nay,' said he, 'my word is for Tete Brece.' And thereon they bore him from that place, and he was in Tete Brece until the end of one year, and during all that time he had speech with no one.

Now upon a certain day before the next Samain, at the end of a year, when the men of Ulster were in the house where Cu Chulainn was, Fergus being at the side-wall, and Conall the Victorious at his head, and Lugaid Red-Stripes at his pillow, and his wife at his feet. When they were there in this manner, a man came to them, and he seated himself near the entrance of the chamber in which Cu Chulainn lay.

'What has brought thee here?' said Conall the Victorious.

'No hard question to answer,' said the man. 'If the man who lies yonder were in health, he would be a good protection to all of Ulster. In the weakness and the sickness in which he now is, so much the more great is the protection that they have from him. I have no fear of any of you,' he said, 'for it is to give to this man a greeting that I come.'

'Welcome to thee, then, and fear nothing,' said the men of Ulster; and the man rose to his feet, and he sang them the following verses:

O Cu Chulainn! of thy illness
Not great will be the length.
They would heal thee if they were here,
The daughters of Aed Abrat.

Thus spoke Liban in Mag Cruach,
By the side of Labraid the Swift:
Love holds Fann's heart;
She longs to be joined to Cu Chulainn.

Goodly in truth would be the day
When Cu Chulainn comes to my land.
If he comes he shall have silver and gold;
He shall have much wine to drink.

Could he but love me enough for that,
Cu Chulainn son of Sualtam!
I have seen him in slumber,
Without his arms, in very truth.

'Tis to Mag Muirthemne thou shouldst go,
On the night of Samain, without injury to thyself.
I will send thee Liban,
To heal thy sickness, o Cu Chulainn!

O Cu Chulainn! of thy illness,
Not great will be the length.
They would heal thee if they were here,
The daughters of Aed Abrat.

'Who art thou, then, thyself?' said the men of Ulster.

'I am Angus, the son of Aed Abrat,' he answered. And the man then left them, nor did any of them know whence it was he had come, nor wither he went.

Then Cu Chulainn sat up, and he spoke to them. 'Fortunate indeed is this!' said the men of Ulster. 'Tell us what it is that has happened to thee.'

'Upon Samain night last year,' he said, 'I indeed saw a vision.' And he told them of all he had seen.

'What should now be done, Father Conchobar?' said Cu Chulainn.

'This hast thou to do,' answered Conchobar. 'Rise and go to the stone where thou wert before.'

Then Cu Chulainn went forth to the stone, and then saw he the woman in the green mantle come to him. 'This is good, o Cu Chulainn!' said she.

'It is no good thing in my thought,' said Cu Chulainn. 'Wherefore camest thou to me last year?'

'It was indeed to do no injury to thee that we came,' said the woman, 'but to seek for thy friendship. I have come to greet thee,' she said, 'from Fann, the daughter of Aed Abrat. Her husband, Manannan mac Lir, has abandoned her, and she has thereon set her love on thee. My own name is Liban, and I have brought to thee a message from my husband, Labraid the Swift Sword-Wielder, that he will give thee the woman Fann in exchange for one day's service to him in battle against Senach Siaborthe, and against Eochaid Iuil, and against Eogan Inber.'

'I am in no fit state,' he said, 'to contend with men today.'

'That will last but a little while,' she said, 'Thou shalt be whole, and all that thou hast lost of thy strength shall be increased to thee. Labraid shall bestow on thee that gift, for he is the best of all warriors that are in the world.'

'Where is it that Labraid dwells?' asked Cu Chulainn.

'In Mag Mell, the Plain of Delight,' said Liban. 'And now I desire to go to that other land,' said she.

'Let Loeg go with thee,' said Cu Chulainn, 'that he may learn of the land from which thou hast come.'

'Let him come, then,' said Liban.

She and Loeg departed after that, and they went forward towards Mag Mell, the place where Fann was. And Liban turned to seek for Loeg, and she placed him beside her shoulder. 'Thou wouldst never go hence, o Loeg!' said Liban, 'wert thou not under a woman's protection.'

'It is not a thing that I have most been accustomed to up to this time,' said Loeg, 'to be under a woman's guard.'

'Shame, and everlasting shame,' said Liban, 'that Cu Chulainn is not where thou art.'

'It were well for me,' answered Loeg, 'if it were indeed he who is here.'

They passed on then, and went forward until they came opposite to the shore of an island, and there they saw a skiff of bronze lying upon the lake before them. They entered into the skiff, and they crossed over to the island, and came to the palace door, and there they saw a man, and he came towards them. And thus spoke Liban to the man whom they saw there:

> Where is Labraid, the swift sword-handler,
> The head of victorious troops?
> Victory is in his strong chariot;
> He stains with red the points of his spears.

And the man replied to her thus:

> Labraid, the swift sword-handler –
> He is not slow; he will be strong.
> They are gathering for the battle;
> They are making ready for the slaughter
> That will fill Mag Fidga.

Celtic necklace of jet.

They entered into the palace, and they saw there thrice fifty couches within the palace, and three times fifty women upon the couches; and the women all bade Loeg welcome, and it was in these words that they addressed him:

> Welcome to thee, o Loeg,
> Because of thy quest;
> Loeg, we also
> Hail thee as our guest!

'What wilt thou do now?' said Liban. 'Wilt thou go on without a delay, and hold speech with Fann?'

'I will go,' he answered, 'if I may know the place where she is.'

'That is no hard matter to tell,' she answered. 'She is in her chamber apart.'

They went there and they greeted Fann, and she welcomed Loeg in the same fashion as the others had done.

Fann was the daughter of Aed Abrat. Aed means fire, and he is the fire of the eye: that is, of the eye's pupil. Fann, moreover, is the name of the tear that runs from the eye; it was on account of the clearness of her beauty that she was so named, for there is nothing else in the world except a tear to which her beauty could be likened.

Now, while they were thus in that place, they heard the rattle of Labraid's chariot as he approached the island, driving across the water. 'The spirit of Labraid is gloomy today,' said Liban. 'I will go and greet him.' And she went on, and she bade welcome to Labraid, and she spoke as follows:

> Hail to Labraid, swift sword-handler!
> Heir to an army − small and armed with javelins.
> He hacks the shields − he shatters the spears,
> He cleaves the bodies − he slaughters free men;
> He seeks for bloodshed − bright is he in the conflict:
> To thee, who war against the hosts, Labraid, hail!
>
> Hail to Labraid, the swift sword-handler!
> Heir to an army − small and armed with javelins.

Labraid did not reply to her, and the lady spoke again thus:

> Hail to Labraid, swift sword-handler!
> Ready in giving − generous to all − eager for combat;
> Scarred thy side − fair thy speech − strong thy hand,
> Kindly in ruling − hardy in judgements − powerful in vengeance.
> He fights off the hosts. Hail, Labraid!
>
> Hail to Labraid, swift handler of the battle-sword!

Labraid still made no answer, and she sang another lay thus:

> Hail, Labraid, swift sword-handler!
> Bravest of warriors – more proud than the sea!
> He routs the armies – he joins the combats;
> He tests the soldiers – he raises up the weak,
> He humbles the strong. Hail, Labraid!
>
> Hail, Labraid, swift sword-handler!

'Thou speakest not rightly, o woman,' said Labraid, and he then addressed her thus:

> There is no pride or arrogance in me, o wife!
> And no deluding spell can weaken my judgement.
> We are going now into a conflict of doubtful issue, decisive and severe,
> Where red swords strike in powerful hands,
> Against the multitudinous and united hosts of Eochaid Iuil.
> There is no presumption in me – no pride and no arrogance in me, o wife!

'Let now thy mind be appeased,' said the woman Liban to him. 'Loeg, the charioteer of Cu Chulainn, is here, and Cu Chulainn has sent word to thee that he will come to join thy hosts.'

Then Labraid bade welcome to Loeg, and he said to him: 'Welcome, o Loeg! for the sake of the lady with whom thou comest, and for the sake of him from whom thou hast come. Go now to thine own land, o Loeg!' said Labraid, ' and Liban shall accompany thee.'

Then Loeg returned to Emain, and he gave news of what he had seen to Cu Chulainn, and to all others beside; and Cu Chulainn rose up, and he passed his hand over his face, and he greeted Loeg brightly, and his mind was strengthened within him for the news that Loeg had brought him.

Now, as to Cu Chulainn, it has to be related thus. He called upon Loeg to come to him. 'Go, o Loeg!' said Cu Chulainn, 'to the place where Emer is, and say to her that fairy women have come upon me, and that they have destroyed my strength; and say also to her that it goes better with me from hour to hour, and bid her to come and see me.'

And the young man Loeg then spoke these words in order to hearten the mind of Cu Chulainn:

> Little indeed is its use to a warrior –
> The bed where he lies in sickness.
> His illness is the work of the fairy folk,
> Of the women of Mag Trogach.

They have beaten thee,
They have put thee into captivity;
They have led thee off the track.
The power of the women has rendered thee impotent.

Awake from the sleep in which thou art fighting
Against beings who are not soldiers;
The hour has come for thee to take thy place
Among heroes who drive their chariots to battle.

Place thyself upon the seat of thy war chariot.
Then will come the chance
To cover thyself with wounds,
To do great deeds.

When Labraid shows his power,
When the splendour of his glory shines,
Then must thou arise,
Then wilt thou be great.

Little indeed is its use to a warrior –
The bed where he lies in sickness.
His illness is the work of the fairy folk,
Of the women of Mag Trogach.

And Loeg, after that heartening, departed, and he went to the place where Emer was, and he told her of the state of Cu Chulainn.

'Ill has it been what thou hast done, o youth!' she said, 'for although thou art known as one who dost wander in the lands where the fairy folk dwell, yet no virtue of healing hast thou found there and brought for the cure of thy lord. Shame upon the men of Ulster!' she said, 'for they have not sought to do a great deed, and to heal him. Yet, had Conchobar thus been fettered, had it been Fergus who lost his sleep, had it been Conall the Victorious to whom wounds had been dealt, Cu Chulainn would have saved them.' And she then sang a song, and in this fashion she sang it:

O Loeg mac Riangabra! alas!'
Thou hast searched fairyland many times in vain;
Thou tarriest long in bringing thence
The healing of the son of Dechtire.

Woe to the high-souled Ulstermen!
Neither foster-father or foster-brother of Cu Chulainn
Has made a search through the wide world
To find the cure for his brave comrade.

If Fergus, foster-father of Cu Chulainn, were under this spell,
And if, to heal him, there was needed the knowledge of a druid,
The son of Dechtire would never take repose
Until Fergus had found a druid who could heal him.

If it were the foster-brother of Cu Chulainn, Conall the Victorious,
Who was afflicted with wounds,
Cu Chulainn would search through the whole world
Until he found a physician to heal him.

If Loegaire the Triumphant
Had been overborne in rugged combat,
Cu Chulainn would have searched through the green meads of all Ireland
To find a cure for the son of Connad mac Iliach.

Alas! sickness seizes upon me, too,
Because of Cu Chulainn, the Hound of Conchobar's smith!
The sickness that I feel at my heart creeps over my whole body!
Would that I might find a physician to heal thee!

Alas! death is at my heart!
For sickness has checked the warrior who rode his chariot across the
    plain,
And now he goes no more
To the assembly of Muirthemne.

Why does he go forth no more from Emain?
It is because of the fairy folk that he lingers.
My voice grows weak and dies.

Month, season, year, all have gone by,
And yet sleep has not taken up its accustomed course.
There is no one by him. Not one fair word
Doth ever come to his ears, o Loeg mac Riangabra.

And, after that she had sung that song, Emer went forward to Emain that
she might visit Cu Chulainn, and she seated herself in the chamber
where Cu Chulainn was, and thus she addressed him: 'Shame upon
thee!' she said, 'to lie thus prostrate for a woman's love! Well may this
long sick-bed of thine cause thee to ail!' And it was in this fashion that
she addressed him, and she chanted this lay:

Arise, hero of Ulster!
Awake joyful and sound.
Look upon the king of Ulster, how great he is!
Long enough hast thou slept.

It is ill sleeping too deep;
It is the weakness that follows defeat;
Sleeping too long is like milk to repletion;
It is the lieutenant of death; it has all death's power.

Awake! Sleep is the repose of the sot;
Throw it off with burning energy.
I have spoken much, but it is love that inspires me.
Arise, hero of Ulster!

Arise, hero of Ulster!
Awake joyful and sound.
Look upon the king of Ulster, how great he is!
Long enough hast thou slept.

And Cu Chulainn at her word stood up, and he passed his hand over his face, and he cast all his heaviness and his weariness away from him, and then he arose, and went on his way before him until he came to the enclosure that he sought. And in that enclosure Liban appeared to him. And Liban spoke to him, and she strove to lead him into fairyland, but, 'What place is that in which Labraid dwells?' said Cu Chulainn.

'It is easy for me to tell thee?' she said:

Labraid's home is over a pure lake,
Where troops of women congregate.
Easy for thee to go there,
If thou wilt know swift Labraid.

His skilled arm strikes down hundreds;
Wise are they who describe his deeds:
Beautifully purple the colours
Which are on the cheeks of Labraid.

He shakes his head like a wolf in the battle
Before the thin blood-stained swords.
He shatters the arms of his impotent enemies;
He shatters the bucklers of the warriors.

'I will not go thither at a woman's invitation,' said Cu Chulainn.

'Let Loeg go, then,' said the woman, 'and let him bring to thee tidings of all that is there.'

'Let him depart, then,' said Cu Chulainn, and Loeg rose up and departed with Liban, and they came to Mag Lauda, and to Bile Buada, and over the fair green of Emain, and over the fair green of Fidga, and in that place dwelt Aed Abrat, and with him his daughters.

Then Fann bade welcome to Loeg, and 'How is it,' said she, 'that Cu Chulainn has not come with thee?'

'It pleased him not,' said Loeg, 'to come at a woman's call. Moreover, he desired to know whether it was indeed from thee that had come the message, and to have full knowledge of everything.'

'It was indeed from me that the message was sent,' she said, ' and let now Cu Chulainn come swiftly to seek us, for it is for today that the strife is set.'

Then Loeg went back to the place where he had left Cu Chulainn, and Liban with him.

'How appears this quest to thee, o Loeg?' said Cu Chulainn.

And Loeg answered, 'In a happy hour shalt thou go,' said he, 'for the battle is set for today.' And it was in this manner that he spake, and described the fairy world thus:

I went in the twinkling of an eye
Into a marvellous country where I had been before.
I reached a cairn of twenty armies,
And there I found Labraid of the long hair.

I found him sitting on the cairn,
A great multitude of arms about him.
On his head his beautiful fair hair
Was decked with an apple of gold.

Although the time was long since my last visit
He recognized me by my five-fold purple mantle.
Said he, 'Wilt thou come with me
Into the house where dwells Failbe the Fair?'

Two kings are in the house,
Failbe the Fair and Labraid.
Three fifties of warriors are about them.
For all their great number they live in the one house.

'Adder stones': ancient British glass ornaments, traditionally associated with the druids.

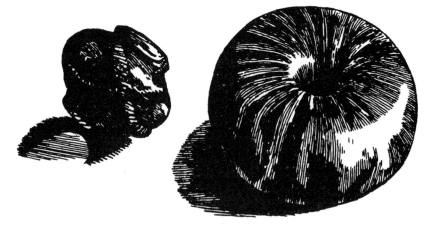

On the right are fifty beds,
And on the beds, as many warriors;
On the left, fifty beds.
And a warrior on every bed.

The beds have round columns,
Beautiful posts, adorned with gold.
They gleam brightly in the light
Which comes from a stone, precious and brilliant.

At the door towards the west
On the side towards the setting sun,
There is a troop of grey horses with dappled manes,
And another troop of horses, purple-brown.

At the door towards the east
Are the trees of purple glass.
From their tops a flock of birds sing a sweetly drawn-out song
For the children who live in the royal stronghold.

At the entrance to the enclosure is a tree
From whose branches there comes beautiful and harmonious music.
It is a tree of silver, which the sun illumines;
It glistens like gold.

There are thrice fifty trees.
At times their leaves mingle, at times not.
Each tree feeds three hundred people
With abundant food, without rind.

There is a well in that noble palace of the fairy-mound.
There you will find thrice fifty splendid cloaks,
With a brooch of shining gold
To fasten each of the cloaks.

There is a cauldron of invigorating mead,
For the use of the inmates of the house.
It never grows less; it is a custom
That is should be full for ever.

There is a woman in the noble palace.
There is no woman like her in Erin.
When she goes forth you see her fair hair.
She is beautiful and endowed with many gifts.

Her words, when she speaks to anyone,
Have a marvellous charm.
She wounds every man to the heart
With the love she inspires.

The noble lady said,
'Who is the youth whom we do not know?
Come hither if it be thou
That art the servant of the warrior of Muirthemne.'

I yielded to her request with reluctance;
I feared for my honour.
She said to me, 'Will he come,
The only son of the excellent Dechtire?'

It is a pity that thou hast not gone, o Cu Chulainn!
Everyone asks for you.
You yourself should see how it is built,
The grand palace that I have seen.

If I owned the whole of Erin,
With supreme sovereignty over its fair inhabitants,
I would give it up – the temptation would be irresistible –
I would go and live in the country where I have just been.

I went in the twinkling of an eye
Into a country where I had been before.
I reached a cairn of twenty armies,
And there I found Labraid of the long hair.

'The quest then is a good one,' said Cu Chulainn.
'It is goodly indeed,' said Loeg, ' and it is right that thou shouldst go to attain it, and all things in that land are good.' And thus further also spoke Loeg, as he told of the loveliness of the fairy dwelling:

They are beautiful women, victorious, never knowing the sorrow of the
    vanquished,
The daughters of Aed Abrat.
The beauty of Fann deserves glittering renown;
No king or queen is her equal.

I repeat what has been said to me:
She is a mortal daughter of Adam, without sin.
The beauty of Fann in our days,
Is beyond comparison.

I saw the glorious warriors
Armed with trenchant weapons,
With garments of bright colours;
These were not the garments of underlings.

I saw the women, joyous at the feast;
I saw the troop of maidens;

I saw the handsome boys
Walking about the trees on the hill.

In the house I heard the musicians
Playing for Fann.
If I had not made haste to go away
I would have got my hurt from that music.

I saw the hill where the house stands.
Ethne Inguba is a fair woman,
But the woman I speak of now,
Would drive entire armies to madness.

And Cu Chulainn, when he had heard that report, went on with Liban
to that land, and he took his chariot with him. And they came to the
island of Labraid, and there Labraid and all the women that were there
bade them welcome, and Fann gave an especial welcome to Cu Chulainn.

'What is there now set for us to do?' said Cu Chulainn.

'No hard matter to answer,' said Labraid. 'We must go forth and make
a circuit about the army.'

They went out then, and they came to the army, and they let their eyes
wander over it; and the host seemed to them to be innumerable. 'Arise
and go hence for the present,' said Cu Chulainn to Labraid, and Labraid
departed, and Cu Chulainn remained confronting the army. And there
were two ravens there who spake, and revealed druid secrets, but the
armies who heard them laughed.

'It must surely be the madman from Ireland who is there,' said the
army. 'It is he whom the ravens would make known to us.' And the
armies chased them away so that they found no resting-place in that
land.

Now at early morn Eochaid Iuil went out in order to bathe his hands
in the spring, and Cu Chulainn saw his shoulder through the hood of his
tunic, and he hurled his spear at him, and he pierced him. And he by
himself slew thirty-three of them, and then Senach Siaborthe assailed
him, and a great fight was fought between them, and Cu Chulainn slew
him. And after that Labraid approached, and he broke before him those
armies.

Then Labraid entreated Cu Chulainn to stay his hand from the
slaying. 'I fear now,' said Loeg, 'that the man will turn his wrath upon
us, for he has not found a combat to suffice him. Go now,' said Loeg, '
and let there be brought three vats of cold water to cool his heat. The
first vat into which he goes will boil over; after he has gone into the
second vat, none will be able to bear the heat of it; after he has gone into
the third vat, its water will have but a moderate heat.'

And when the women saw Cu Chulainn's return, Fann sang thus:

Stately the charioteer that steps the road;
If he be beardless it is because he is young.
Splendid the course he drives over the plain,
At eve on Aenach Fidgai.

There is in each of his two cheeks
A red dimple like red blood,
A green dimple, a brown dimple,
A crimson dimple of light colour.

There are seven lights in his eye –
It is a fact not to be left unspoken –
Eyebrows brown, of noblest set,
Eyelashes of chafer black.

He outstrips all men in every slaughter;
He traverses the battle to the place of danger;
There is not one with a high hardy blade,
Not one like Cu Chulainn.

Cu Chulainn it is that comes hither,
The young champion from Muirthemne;
They who have brought him from afar
Are the daughters of Aed Abrat.

Dripping blood in long red streams,
To the sides of lofty spears he brings;
Haughty, proud, high for valour,
Woe be to him against whom he becomes angered.

Liban, moreover, bade a welcome to Cu Chulainn, and she sang as follows:

Welcome to Cu Chulainn;
Relieving king;
A great prince of Mag Muirthemne;
Great his noble mind;
A battle-victorious champion;
A strong valour-stone;
Blood-red of anger;
Ready to arrange the champions of valour of Ulster;
Beautiful his complexion;
Dazzler of the eyes to maidens;
He is welcome.

'Tell us now of the deeds thou hast done, o Cu Chulainn!' cried Liban, and Cu Chulainn replied to her thus:

I threw a cast of my spear
Into the court of Eogan Inber,
I do not know – path of fame –
Whether it is good I have done, or evil.

A host fair, red-complexioned, on backs of steeds,
They pierced me upon all sides;
The people of Manannan son of Lir,
Invoked by Eogan Inber.

I heard the groan of Eochaid Iuil;
It is in good friendship his lips speak.
If the man has spoken true, it certainly won the battle,
The throw that I threw.

Now, after all these things had passed, Cu Chulainn slept with Fann, and
he abode for a month in her company, and at the end of the month he
came to bid her farewell.

'Tell me,' she said, 'to what place I may go for our tryst, and I will be
there.' And they made tryst at the yew tree by the strand that is known
as Iubar Cinn Trachta [Newry].

Now word was brought to Emer of that tryst, and knives were
whetted by Emer to slay the fairy woman; and she came to the place of
the tryst, and fifty women were with her. And there she found Cu
Chulainn and Loeg, and they were engaged in the chess-play, so that they
did not perceive the women's approach. But Fann marked it, and she
cried out to Loeg: 'Look now, o Loeg!' she said, ' and mark that sight that
I see.'

'What sight is that of which thou speakest?' said Loeg, and he looked
and saw it, and thus it was that Fann addressed him:

Loeg! look behind thee!
    Close at hand
Wise, well-ranked women
    Press on us;
Bright on each bosom
    Shines the gold clasp;
Knives, with green edges
    Whetted, they hold.
As for the slaughter chariot chiefs race,
Comes Forgall's daughter; changed is her countenance.

'Have no fear,' said Cu Chulainn, 'thou shalt meet no foe;
Enter thou my strong car, with its bright seat:
I will set thee before me, will guard thee from harm
Against women, that swarm from Ulster's four quarters:

Though the daughter of Forgall vows war against thee,
Though her dear foster-sisters she rouses against thee,
Bold Emer will dare no deed of destruction,
Though she rageth against thee, for I will protect thee.'

Moreover, to Emer he said:

I avoid thee, o lady, as heroes
    Avoid to meet friends in battle;
The hard spear thy hand shakes cannot injure,
    Nor the blade of thy thin gleaming knife;
For the wrath that rages within thee
    Is but weak, nor can cause me fear:
It were hard if the war my might wages
    Must be quenched by a weak woman's power.

'Speak! and tell me, Cu Chulainn,' said Emer,
    'Why thy wouldst lay this shame on my head?
I stand dishonoured before the women of Ulster,
And all women who dwell in Erin,
    And all folk who love honour beside:
Though I came on thee secretly,
    Though I remain oppressed by thy might,
And though great is thy pride in the battle,
    If thou leavest me, naught is thy gain:
Why, dear youth, dost thou make such attempt?'

'Speak thou, Emer, and say,' said Cu Chulainn,
    'Should I not remain with this lady?
For she is fair, pure and bright, and well skilled,
A fit mate for a monarch, filled with beauty,
    And can ride the waves of ocean:
She is lovely in countenance, lofty in race,
And skilled in handicraft, can do fine needlework,
    Has a mind that can guide with firmness.'

'Truly,' answered Emer, 'the woman to whom thou dost cling is in no way better than am I myself! Yet fair seems all that's red; what's new seems glittering; and bright what's set o'erhead; and sour are things well known! Men worship what they lack; and what they have seems weak; in truth thou hast all the wisdom of the time! O youth!' she said, ' once we dwelled in honour together, and we would so dwell again, if only I could find favour in thy sight!' And her grief weighed heavily upon her.

'By my word,' said Cu Chulainn, 'thou dost find favour, and thou shalt find it as long as I am in life.'

'Desert me, then!' cried Fann.

'No,' said Emer, 'it is more fitting that I should be the deserted one.'

'Not so, indeed,' said Fann. 'It is I who must go, and danger rushes upon me from afar.' And an eagerness for lamentation seized upon Fann, and her soul was great within her, for it was shame to her to be deserted and straightway to return to her home. Moreover, the mighty love that she bore to Cu Chulainn was tumultuous in her, and in this fashion she lamented, and lamenting sang this song:

I it is that will go on the journey;
I give assent with great affliction;
Though there is a man of equal fame,
I would prefer to remain.

I would rather be here,
To be subject to thee, without grief,
Than to go, though you may wonder at it,
To the sunny place of Aed Abrat.

O Emer! the man is thine,
And well mayst thou wear him, thou good woman –
What my arm cannot reach,
That I am forced to wish well.

Many were the men that were asking for me,
Both in the court and in the wilderness;
Never with those did I hold a meeting,
Because I it was that was righteous.

Woe! to give love to a person,
If he does not take notice of it;
It is better for a person to turn away
Unless he is loved as he loves.

With fifty women hast thou come hither,
O Emer of the yellow hair,
To capture Fann – it was not well –
And to kill her in the misery.

There are thrice fifty, during my days,
Of women, beautiful and unwedded,
With me in my court together;
They would not abandon me.

Now upon this it was discerned by Manannan that Fann the daughter of Aed Abrat was engaged in unequal warfare with the women of Ulster, and that she was like to be left by Cu Chulainn. And thereon Manannan came from the east to seek for Fann, and he was perceived by her, nor was there any other conscious of his presence saving Fann alone.

And when she saw Manannan, Fann was seized by great bitterness of mind and by grief, and being thus, she made this song:

Behold the valiant son of Lir,
From the plains of Eogan Inber –
Manannan, lord over the world's fair hills,
There was a time when he was dear to me.

Even if today he were nobly constant,
My mind loves not jealousy.
Affection is a subtle thing;
It makes its way without labour.

One day I was with the son of Lir,
In the sunny palace of Dun Inber;
We then thought, without doubt,
That we should never be separated.

When Manannan, the great one, espoused me,
I was a worthy wife for him;
For his life he could not win from me
The odd game at chess.

When Manannan the great married me,
I was a wife worthy of him;
A wristband of doubly-tested gold
He gave to me as the price of my blushes.

I had with me at going over the sea
Fifty maidens of many gifts.
I gave to them fifty men,
Without reproach, as their companions.

Four fifties, without deceit,
That was the assembly of one house;
Twice fifty men, happy and perfect,
Twice fifty women, fair and healthy.

I see coming over the sea hither –
No erring person sees him –
The horseman of the crested wave;
He stays not on his long boats.

At thy coming, no one yet sees,
Anyone but a dweller in the fairy-mound;
Thy good sense is magnified by every gentle host,
Though they be far away from thee.

As for me, I would have cause for anger,
Because the minds of women are silly;
The person whom I loved exceedingly
Has placed me here at a disadvantage.

I bid thee farewell, o beautiful Cu;
We depart from thee with a good heart;
Though we return not, be thy good will with us;
Everything is good, compared with going away.

It is now time for me to take my departure;
There is a person to whom it is not a grief;
It is, however, a great disgrace,
O Loeg, son of Riangabar.

I shall go with my own husband,
Because he will not show my disobedience.
Now that you may not say it is a secret departure,
If you desire it, now behold me.

Then Fann rose behind Manannan as he passed, and Manannan greeted her. 'O woman!' he said, 'which wilt thou do? Wilt thou depart with me, or abide here until Cu Chulainn comes to thee?'

'In truth,' answered Fann, 'either of the two of you would be a fitting husband to adhere to, and neither of you is better than the other. Yet, Manannan, it is with thee that I go, nor will I wait for Cu Chulainn, for he has betrayed me; and there is another matter, moreover, that weigheth with me, o noble prince!' said she, 'and that is that thou hast no consort who is of worth equal to thine, but such a one hath Cu Chulainn already.'

And Cu Chulainn saw Fann as she went from him to Manannan, and he cried out to Loeg: 'What does this mean that I see?'

''Tis no hard matter to answer,' said Loeg. 'Fann is going away with Manannan mac Lir, since she hath not pleased thee!'

Then Cu Chulainn bounded three times high into the air, and he made three great leaps towards the south, and thus he came to Tara Luachra, and there he abode for a long time, having no meat and no drink, dwelling upon the mountains, and sleeping upon the high-road that runs through the midst of Luachra.

Then Emer went on to Emain, and there she sought out king Conchobar, and she told him of Cu Chulainn's state, and Conchobar sent out his learned men and his people of skill, and the druids of Ulster, to find Cu Chulainn, and to bind him fast, and bring him with them to Emain. And Cu Chulainn tried to kill the people of skill, but they chanted wizard and fairy spells against him, and they bound fast his feet and his hands until he came a little to his senses. Then he begged for a drink at their hands, and the druids gave him a drink of forgetfulness, so that afterwards he had no more remembrance of Fann nor of anything else that he had then done; and they also gave him a drink of forgetfulness to Emer that she might forget her jealousy, for her state was in no way better than the state of Cu Chulainn. And Manannan shook his cloak between Cu Chulainn and Fann, so that they might never meet together again throughout eternity.

Bronze swords.

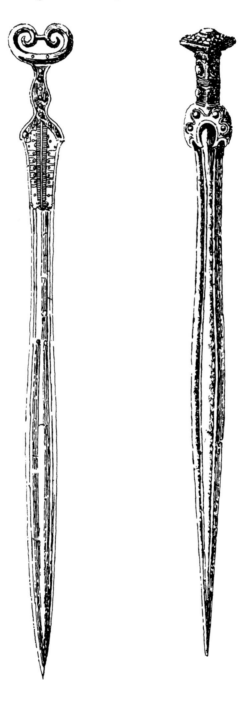

6 the Marriage of Sir Gawain
(England)

Celtic legends were also preserved as poetry, both oral and literary. The following poem, in ballad style, is from Thomas Percy's *Reliques of Ancient English Poetry* (1765), reworked by Percy from an older set of fragments. Gawain, one of the Round Table knights, is drawn from an older Celtic hero and deity, as is shown by John Matthews in his book *Gawain*, published in 1990 by Aquarian Press.

The metrical version of Gawain's marriage is matched by some ballads and tales from oral tradition. The theme is one which masks the ancient transformations of the Goddess, who is at once hag, mother and maiden.

PART THE FIRST

KING Arthur lives in merry Carleile,
  And seemely is to see;
And there with him Queene Guenever,
  That bride soe bright of blee.

And there with him queene Guenever,
  That bride soe bright in bowre:
And all his barons about him stoode,
  That were both stiffe and stowre.

The king a royale Christmasse kept,
  With mirth and princelye cheare;
To him repaired many a knighte,
  That came both farre and neare.

And when they were to dinner sette,
    And cups went freely round:
Before them came a faire damsèlle,
    And knelt upon the ground.

A boone, a boone, O Kinge Arthùre,
    I beg a boone of thee;
Avenge me of a carlish knighte,
    Who hath shent my love and mee.

At Tearne-Wadling his castle stands,
    Near to that lake so fair,
And proudlye rise the battlements,
    And streamers deck the air.

Noe gentle knighte, nor ladye gay,
    May pass that castle-walle:
But from that foule discurteous knighte,
    Mishappe will them befalle.

Hee's twyce the size of commen men,
    Wi' thewes, and sinewes stronge,
And on his backe he bears a clubbe,
    That is both thicke and longe.

This grimme baròne 'twas our harde happe,
    But yester morne to see;
When to his bowre he bare my love,
    And sore misused mee.

And when I told him, King Arthùre
    As lyttle shold him spare;
Goe tell, sayd hee, that cuckold kinge,
    To meete mee if he dare.

Upp then sterted King Arthùre,
    And sware by hille and dale,
He ne'er wolde quitt that grimme baròne,
    Till he had made him quail.

Goe fetch my sword Excalibar;
    Goe saddle mee my steede;
Nowe, by my faye, that grimme baròne
    Shall rue this ruthfulle deede.

And when he came to Tearne Wadlinge
    Benethe the castle walle:
'Come forth; come forth; thou proude baròne,
    Or yielde thyself my thralle.'

On magicke grounde that castle stoode,
    And fenc'd with many a spelle:
Noe valiant knighte could tread thereon,
    But straite his courage felle.

Forth then rush'd that carlish knight,
    King Arthur felte the charme:
His sturdy sinewes lost their strengthe,
    Downe sunke his feeble arme.

Nowe yield thee, yield thee, King Arthùre,
    Now yielde thee unto mee:
Or fighte with mee, or lose thy lande,
    Noe better termes maye bee,

Unlesse thou sweare upon the rood,
    And promise on thy faye,
Here to returne to Tearne-Wadling,
    Upon the new-yeare's daye:

And bringe me worde what thing it is
    All women moste desyre:
This is thy ransome, Arthur, he sayes,
    Ile have noe other hyre.

King Arthur then helde up his hande,
    And sware upon his faye,
Then tooke his leave of the grimme baròne,
    And faste hee rode awaye.

And he rode east, and he rode west,
    And did of all inquyre,
What thing it is all women crave,
    And what they most desyre.

Some told him riches, pompe, or state;
    Some rayment, fine and brighte;
Some told him mirthe; some flatterye;
    And some a jollye knighte.

In letters all King Arthur wrote,
    And seal'd them with his ringe:
But still his minde was helde in doubte,
    Each tolde a different thinge.

As ruthfulle he rode over a more,
    He saw a ladye sette
Betweene an oke, and a green holléye,
    All clad in red scarlette.

Her nose was crookt and turnd outwàrde,
    Her chin stoode all awrye;
And where as sholde have been her mouthe,
    Lo! there was set her eye:

Her haires, like serpents, clung aboute
    Her cheekes of deadlye hewe:
A worse-form'd ladye than she was,
    No man mote ever viewe.

To hail the king in seemelye sorte
    This ladye was fulle faine:
But King Arthùre all sore amaz'd,
    No aunswere made againe.

What wight art thou, the ladye sayd,
    That wilt not speake to mee;
Sir, I may chance to ease thy paine,
    Though I bee foule to see.

If thou wilt ease my paine, he sayd,
    And helpe me in my neede;
Ask what thou wilt, thou grimme ladyè,
    And it shall bee thy meede.

O sweare mee this upon the roode,
    And promise on thy faye;
And here the secrette I will telle,
    That shall thy ransome paye.

King Arthur promis'd on his faye,
    And sware upon the roode:
The secrette then the ladye told,
    As lightlye well shee cou'de.

Now this shall be my paye, sir king,
    And this my guerdon bee,
That some young fair and courtlye knight,
    Thou bringe to marrye mee.

Fast then pricked King Arthùre
    Ore hille, and dale, and downe:
And soone he founde the barone's bowre:
    And soone the grimme baroùne.

He bare his clubbe upon his backe,
    Hee stoode bothe stiffe and stronge;
And, when he had the letters reade,
    Awaye the lettres flunge.

Nowe yield thee, Arthur, and thy lands,
    All forfeit unto mee;
For this is not thy paye, sir king,
    Nor may thy ransome bee.

Yet hold thy hand, thou proud baròne,
    I pray thee hold thy hand;
And give me leave to speake once more
    In reskewe of my land.

This morne, as I came over a more,
    I saw a lady sette
Betwene an oke, and a greene hollèye,
    All clad in red scarlètte.

Shee sayes, all women will have their wille,
    This is their chief desyre;
Now yield, as thou art a barone true,
    That I have payd mine hyre.

An earlye vengeaunce light on her!
    The carlish baron swore:
Shee was my sister tolde thee this,
    And shee's a mishapen whore.

But here I will make mine avowe,
    To do her as ill a turne:
For an ever I may that foule thiefe gette,
    In a fyre I will her burne.

PART THE SECONDE

Homewarde pricked King Arthùre,
    And a wearye man was hee;
And soone he mette Queene Guenever,
    That bride so blight of blee.

What newes! what newes! thou noble king,
    Howe, Arthur, has thou sped?
Where hast thou hung the carlish knighte?
    And where bestow'd his head?

Bronze sword from
Arthur's Seat, Edinburgh.

The carlish knight is safe for mee,
    And free fro mortal harme:
On magicke ground his castle stands,
    And fenc'd with many a charme.

To bowe to him I was fulle faine,
    And yielde me to his hand:
And but for a lothly ladye, there
    I sholde have lost my land.

And nowe this fills my hearte with woe,
    And sorrowe of my life;
I swore a yonge and courtlye knight,
    Sholde marry her to his wife.

Then bespake him Sir Gawàine,
    That was ever a gentle knighte:
That lothly ladye I will wed;
    Therefore be merrye and lighte.

Nowe naye, nowe naye, good Sir Gawàine;
    My sister's sonne yee bee;
This lothlye ladye's all too grimme,
    And all too foule for yee.

Her nose is crookt, and turn'd outwàrde;
    Her chin stands all awrye;
A worse form'd ladye than she was
    Was never seen with eye.

What though her chin stand all awrye,
    And shee be foul to see;
I'll marry her, unkle, for thy sake,
    And I'll thy ransome bee.

Nowe thankes, nowe thankes, good Sir Gawàine;
    And a blessing thee betyde!
To-morrow wee'll have knights and squires,
    And wee'll goe fetch thy bride.

And wee'll have hawkes and we'll have houndes,
    To cover our intent;
And wee'll away to the greene forèst,
    As wee a hunting went.

Sir Lancelot, Sir Stephen bolde,
    They rode with them that daye,
And foremoste of the companye
    There rode the stewarde Kaye:

Soe did Sir Banier and Sir Bore,
    And eke Sir Garratte keene;
Sir Tristram, too, that gentle knight,
    To the forest freshe and greene.

And when they came to the greene forrèst,
    Beneathe a faire holley tree
There sate that ladye in red scarlètte
    That unseemelye was to see.

Sir Kay beheld that lady's face,
    And looked upon her sweere;
Whoever kisses that ladye, he sayes,
    Of his kisse he stands in feare.

Sir Kay beheld that ladye againe,
    And looked upon her snout;
Whoever kisses that ladye, he sayes,
    Of his kisse he stands in doubt.

Peace, brother Kay, sayde Sir Gawàine,
    And amend thee of thy life:
For there is a knight amongst us all,
    Must marry her to his wife.

What marry this foule queane, quoth Kay,
    I' the devil's name anone;
Gett mee a wife wherever I maye,
    In sooth shee shall be none.

Then some tooke up their hawkes in haste,
    And some took up their houndes;
And sayd they wolde not marry her,
    For cities, nor for townes.

Then bespake him King Arthùre,
    And sware there by this daye;
For a little foule sighte and mislikinge,
    Yee shall not saye her naye.

Peace, lordings, peace; Sir Gawàine sayd;
    Nor make debate and strife;
This lothlye ladye I will take,
    And marry her to my wife.

Nowe thankes, nowe thankes, good Sir Gawaine,
    And a blessing be thy meede!
For as I am thine own ladyè,
    Thou never shalt rue this deede.

Then up they took that lothly dame,
    And home anone they bringe;
And there Sir Gawaine he her wed,
    And married her with a ringe.

And when they were in wed-bed laid,
    And all were done away:
'Come turne to mee, mine owne wed-lord,
    Come turne to mee I praye.'

Sir Gawaine scant could lift his head,
    For sorrowe and for care;
When, lo! instead of that lothelye dame,
    Hee sawe a young ladye faire.

Bell shrine with
Celtic motifs.

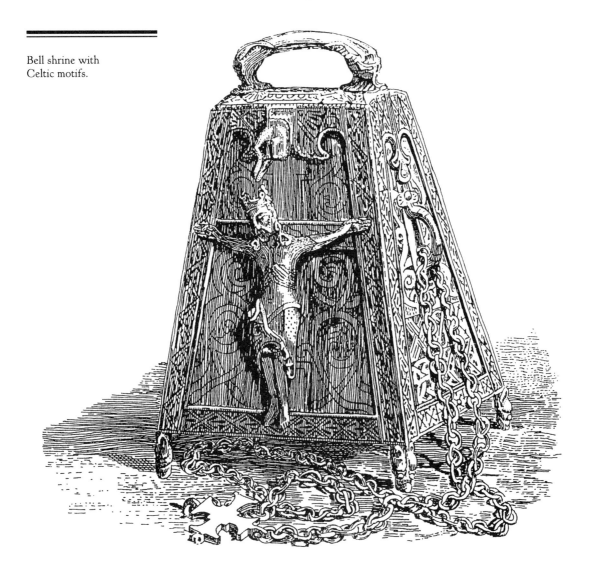

Sweet blushes stayn'd her rud-red cheeke,
    Her eyen was blacke as sloe:
The ripening cherrye swellde her lippe,
    And all her necke was snowe.

Sir Gawaine kiss'd that lady faire,
    Lying upon the sheete:
And swore, as he was a true knighte,
    The spice was never soe sweete.

Sir Gawaine kiss'd that lady brighte,
    Lying there by his side:
'The fairest flower is not soe faire:
    Thou never can'st bee my bride.'

I am thy bride, mine owne deare lorde,
    The same whiche thou didst knowe,
That was soe lothlye, and was wont
    Upon the wild more to goe.

Nowe, gentle Gawaine, chuse, quoth shee,
    And make thy choice with care;
Whether by night, or else by daye,
    Shall I be foule or faire?

'To have thee foule still in the night,
    When I with thee should playe!
I had rather farre, my lady deare,
    To have thee foule by daye.'

What when gaye ladyes goe with their lordes
    To drinke the ale and wine;
Alas! then I must hide myself,
    I must not goe with mine!

'My faire ladyè,' Sir Gawaine sayd,
    'I yield me to thy skille;
Because thou art mine owne ladyè
    Thou shalt have all thy wille.'

Nowe blessed be thou, sweete Gawàine,
    And the daye that I thee see;
For as thou seest mee at this time,
    Soe shall I ever bee.

My father was an aged knighte,
    And yet it chanced soe,
He tooke to wife a false ladyè.
    Whiche broughte me to this woe.

Shee witch'd mee, being a faire yonge maide,
  In the green forèst to dwelle;
And there to abide in lothlye shape,
  Most like a fiend of helle.

Midst mores and mosses; woods, and wilds;
  To lead a lonesome life:
Till some yong faire and courtlye knighte
  Wolde marrye me to his wife:

Nor fully to gaine mine owne trewe shape,
  Such was her devillish skille;
Until he wolde yielde to be rul'd by mee,
  And let mee have all my wille.

She witch'd my brother to a carlish boore,
  And made him stiffe and stronge;
And built him a bowre on magicke grounde,
  To live by rapine and wronge.

But now the spelle is broken throughe,
  And wronge is turnde to righte;
Henceforth I shall bee a faire ladyè,
  And hee be a gentle knighte.

7

the Warrior of the Red Shield
(Scotland)

This story, belonging to the oral tradition, was written down from the words of a Gaelic story-teller, John MacGilvray, of Colonsay, in the West Highlands, and published in J.F. Campbell's *Popular Tales of the Western Highlands* in 1860. Though this story was collected in Scotland centuries after the Cuchulainn material was first written down in eighth-century Ireland, the ambience of 'The Warrior of the Red Shield' is very close to the heroic, apparently Bronze Age, setting of Irish epics.

The telling of such stories was a lengthy social event, with families gathering to hear tales that could last not merely for hours but for nights and days. 'The Warrior of the Red Shield' is, therefore, a fairly short offering. Nevertheless, it is packed with wonders, magic and mysterious obligations. The *geas* or obligation plays a major role in Celtic legend, and brings about the ultimate downfall of many a hero, including Cuchulainn. In this story the warriors seem to represent the energies of the Elements of Four Directions, seeking to bring balance about by fulfilling certain obligations connected to kingship.

A number of the Gaelic terms in the old stories are almost impossible to translate as they have many levels of meaning. In certain cases story-tellers themselves used words whose meaning they did not know but they had been handed down and preserved in tradition. A few of these words have been left intact in the translation that appears here.

*T*HERE was before now a king of Erinn, and he went himself, and his people, and his warriors, and his nobles, and his great gentles, to the hill of hunting and game. They sat on a hillock coloured green colour, where the sun would rise early, and where she would set late.

Said the one of swifter mouth than the rest. 'Who now in the four quarters of the universe would have the heart to put an affront and disgrace on the King of Erinn, and he in the midst of the people, and the warriors, great gentles, and nobles of his own realm.'

'Are ye not silly,' said the king. 'He might come, one who should put an affront and disgrace on me, and that ye could not pluck the worst hair in his beard out of it.'

It was thus it was. They saw the shadow of a shower coming from the western quarter, and going to the eastern quarter; and a rider of a black filly coming cheerily after it.

> As it were a warrior on the mountain shore,
> As a star over sparklings,
> As a great sea over little pools,
> As a smith's smithy coal
> Being quenched at the river side;
> So would seem the men and women of the world beside him,
> In figure, in shape, in form, and in visage.

Then he spoke to them in the understanding, quieting, truly wise words of real knowledge; and before there was any more talk between them, he put over his fist and he struck the king between the mouth and the nose, and he drove out three of his teeth, and he caught them in his fist, and he put them in his pouch, and he went away.

'Did not I say to you,' said the king, 'that one might come who should put an affront and disgrace on me, and that you could not pluck the worst hair in his beard out of it!'

Then his big son, the Warrior of the Cairn, swore that he wouldn't eat meat, and that he wouldn't drink draught, and that he would not hearken to music, until he should take off the warrior that struck the fist on the king, the head that designed to do it.

'Well,' said the Warrior of the Sword, the very same for me, until I take the hand that struck the fist on the king from off the shoulder.

There was one man with them there in the company, whose name was Mac an Earraich uaine ri Gaisge, The Son of the Green Spring by Valour. 'The very same for me,' said he, 'until I take out of the warrior who struck the fist on the king, the heart that thought on doing it.'

'Thou cruel creature!' said the Warrior of the Cairn, 'what should bring thee with us? When we should go to valour, thou wouldst turn to weakness; thou wouldst find death in boggy moss, or in rifts of rock, or in a land of holes, or in the shadow of a wall, or in some place.'

'Be that as it will, but I will go,' said the Son of the Green Spring by Valour.

The king's two sons went away. Glance that the Warrior of the

Cairns gave behind him, he sees the Son of the Green Spring by Valour following them.

'What,' said the Warrior of the Cairn to the Warrior of the Sword, ' shall we do to him?'

'Do,' said the Warrior of the Sword, ' sweep his head off.'

'Well,' said the Warrior of the Cairn, 'we will not do that; but there is a great crag of stone up here, and we will bind him to it.'

'I am willing to do that same,' said the other.

They bound him to the crag of stone to leave him till he should die, and they went away. Glance that the Warrior of the Cairn gave behind him again, he sees him coming and the crag upon him.

'Dost thou not see that one coming again, and the crag upon him!' said the Warrior of the Cairn to the Warrior of the Sword. 'What shall we do to him?'

'It is to sweep the head off him, and not let him come further,' said the Warrior of the Sword.

'We will not do that,' said the Warrior of the Cairn, 'but we will turn back and loose the crag off him. It is but a sorry matter for two full heroes like us; though he should be with us, he will make a man to polish a shield, or blow a fire heap or something.'

They loosed him, and they let him come with them. Then they went down to the shore; then they got the ship, which was called *An Iubhrach Bhallach*, the speckled barge.

> They put her out, and they gave her prow to sea, and her stern to shore.
> They hoisted the speckled, flapping, bare-topped sails
> Up against the tall, tough, splintery masts.
> They had a pleasant little breeze as they might choose themselves,
> Would bring heather from the hill, leaf from grove, willow from its roots,
> Would put thatch of the houses in furrows of the ridges.
> The day that neither the son nor the father could do it,
> That same was neither little nor much for them,
> But using it and taking it as it might come,
> The sea plunging and surging,
> The red sea the blue sea lashing
> And striking hither and thither about her planks.
> The whorled dun whelk that was down on the ground of the ocean.
> Would give a snag on her gunwale and crack on her floor,
> She would cut a slender oaten straw with the excellence of her going.

They gave three days driving her thus. 'I myself am growing tired of this,' said the Warrior of the Cairn to the Warrior of the Sword. 'It seems to me time to get news from the mast.'

'Thou thyself are the most greatly beloved here, o Warrior of the Cairn, and shew that thou wilt have honour going up; and if thou goest not up, we will have the more sport with thee,' said the Son of the Green Spring by Valour.

Up went the Warrior of the Cairn with a rush, and he fell down clatter in a faint on the deck of the ship.

'It is ill thou hast done,' said the Warrior of the Sword.

'Let us see if thyself be better. And if thou be better, it will be shewn that thou wilt have more will to go on; or else we will have the more sport with thee,' said the Son of the Great Spring by Valour.

Up went the Warrior of the Sword, and before he had reached but half the mast, he began squealing and squealing, and he could neither go up nor come down.

'Thou hast done as thou wert asked; and thou hast shewed that thou hadst the more respect for going up; and now thou canst not go up, neither canst thou come down! No warrior was I nor half a warrior, and the esteem of a warrior was not mine at the time of leaving; I was to find death in boggy moss, or in rifts of rock, or in the shade of a wall, or in some place; and it were no effort for me to bring news from the mast.'

'Thou great hero!' said the Warrior of the Cairn, 'try it.'

'A great hero am I this day, but not when leaving the town,' said the Son of the Green Spring by Valour.

He measured a spring from the ends of his spear to the points of his toes, and he was up in the cross-trees in a twinkling.

'What art thou seeing?' said the Warrior of the Cairn.

'It is too big for a crow, and it is too little for land,' said he.

'Stay, as thou hast to try if thou canst know what it is,' said they to him; and he stayed so for a while.

'What art thou seeing now?' said they to him.

'It is an island and a hoop of fire about it, flaming at either end; and I think that there is not one warrior in the great world that will go over the fire,' said he.

'Unless two heroes such as we go over it,' said they.

'I think that it was easier for you to bring news from the mast than to go in there,' said he.

'It is no reproach!' said the Warrior of the Cairn.

'It is not; it is truth,' said the Son of the Green Spring by Valour.

They reached the windward side of the fire, and they went on shore; and they drew the speckled barge up her own seven lengths on grey grass, with her mouth under her, where the scholars of a big town could neither make ridicule, scoffing or mockery of her. They blew up a fire heap, and they gave three days and three nights resting their weariness.

At the end of the three days they began at sharpening their arms.

'I,' said the Warrior of the Cairn, 'am getting tired of this. It seems to me time to get news from the isle.'

'Thou art thyself the most greatly beloved here,' said the Son of the

Green Spring by Valour, 'and go the first and try what is the best news that thou canst bring to us.'

The Warrior of the Cairn went and he reached the fire; and he tried to leap over it, and down he went into it to his knees, and he turned back, and there was not a slender hair or skin between his knees and his ankles, that was not in a crumpled fold about the mouth of the shoes.

'He's bad, he's bad,' said the Warrior of the Sword.

'Let us see if thou art better thyself,' said the Son of the Green Spring by Valour. 'Shew that thou wilt have the greater honour going on, or else we will have the more sport with thee.'

The Warrior of the Sword went, and he reached the fire; and he tried to leap over it, and down he went into it to the thick end of the thigh; and he turned back, and there was no slender hair or skin between the thick end of the thigh and the ankle that was not in a crumpled fold about the mouth of the shoes.

'Well,' said the Son of the Green Spring by Valour, 'no warrior was I leaving the town, in your esteem; and if I had my choice of arms and armour of all that there are in the great world, it were no effort for me to bring news from the isle.'

'If we had that thou shouldst have it,' said the Warrior of the Cairn.

'Warrior of the Cairn, thine own arms and armour are the second that I would rather be mine of all in the great world, although thou thyself art not the second best warrior in it,' said the Son of the Green Spring by Valour.

'It is my own arms and array that are easiest to get,' said the Warrior of the Cairn, ' and thou shalt have them; but I should like that thou wouldst be so good as to tell me what other arms or array are better than mine.'

'There are the arms and array of the Great Son of the sons of the universe, who struck the fist on thy father,' said the Son of the Green Spring by Valour.

The Warrior of the Cairn put off his arms and array; and the Son of the Green Spring by Valour went into his arms and his array.

> He went into his harness of battle and hard combat,
> As was a shirt of smooth yellow silk and gauze stretched on his breast;
> His coat, his kindly coat, above the kindly covering;
> His boss covered; hindering sharp-pointed shield on his left hand,
> His head-dress a helm of hard combat,
> To cover his crown and his head top,
> To go in the front of the fray and the fray long-lasting;
> His heroes hard slasher in his right hand,
> A sharp surety knife against his waist.

He raised himself up to the top of the shore; and there was no turf he would cast behind his heels, that was not as deep as a turf that the bread-covering tree would cast when deepest it would be ploughing. He reached the circle of fire; he leapt from the points of his spear to the points of his toes over the fire.

Then there was the very finest isle that ever was seen from the beginning of the universe to the end of eternity. He went up about the island, and he saw a yellow bare hill in the midst. He raised himself up against the hill. There was a treasure of a woman sitting on the hill, and a great youth with his head on her knee, and asleep. He spoke to her in instructed, eloquent, true, wise, soft, maiden words of true knowledge. She answered in like words; and if they were no better, they were not a whit worse, for the time.

'A man of thy seeming is a treasure for me; and if I had a right to thee, thou shouldst not leave the island,' said the little treasure.

'If a man of my seeming were a treasure for thee, thou wouldst tell me what were waking for that youth,' said the Son of the Green Spring by Valour.

'It is to take off the point of his little finger,' said she.

He laid a hand on the sharp surety knife that was against his waist, and he took the little finger off him from the root. That made the youth neither shrink nor stir.

'Tell me what is waking for the youth, or else there are two off whom

I will take the heads, thyself and the youth,' said the Son of the Green Spring by Valour.

'Waking for him,' said she, 'is a thing that thou canst not do, nor any one warrior in the great world, but the Warrior of the Red Shield, of whom it was in the prophecies that he should come to this island, and strike yonder crag of stone on this man in the rock of his chest; and he is unbaptized till he does that.'

He heard this that such was in the prophecy for him, and he unnamed. A fist upon manhood, a fist upon strengthening, and a fist upon power went into him. He raised the crag in his two hands, and he struck it on the youth in the rock of his chest. The one who was asleep gave a slow stare of his two eyes and he looked at him.

'Aha!' said the one who was asleep, 'hast thou come, Warrior of the Red Shield. It is this day that thou has the name; thou wilt not stand long to me.'

'Two thirds of thy fear be on thyself, and one on me,' said the Warrior of the Red Shield; 'thou wilt not stand long to me.'

In each other's grips they went, and they were hard belabouring each other till the mouth of dusk and lateness was. The Warrior of the Red Shield thought that he was far from his friends and near his foe; he gave him that little light lift, and he struck him against the earth; the thumb of his foot gave a warning to the root of his ear, and he swept the head off him.

'Though it be I who have done this, it was not I who promised it,' said he.

He took the hand off him from the shoulder, and he took the heart from his chest, and he took the head off the neck; he put his hand in the dead warrior's pouch, and he found three teeth of an old horse in it, and with the hurry took them for the king's teeth, and he took them with him; and he went to a tuft of wood, and he gathered a withy, and he tied on it the hand and the heart and the head.

'Whether wouldst thou rather stay here on this island by thyself, or go with me?' said he to the little treasure.

'I would rather go with thee thyself than with all the men of earth's mould together,' said the little treasure.

He raised her with him on the shower top of his shoulders, and on the burden-bearing part of his back, and he went to the fire. He sprang over with the little treasure upon him. He sees the Warrior of the Cairn and the Warrior of the Sword coming to meet him, rage and fury in their eyes.

'What great warrior,' said they, 'was that after thee there, and returned when he saw two heroes like us?'

'Here's for you,' said he, 'this little treasure of a woman, and the three teeth of your father; and the head, and hand, and heart of the one who struck the fist on him. Make a little stay and I will return, and I will not leave a shred of a tale in the island.'

He went away back; and at the end of a while he cast an eye behind him, and he sees them and the speckled barge playing him ocean hiding.

'Death wrappings upon yourselves!' said he, 'a tempest of blood about your eyes, the ghost of your hanging be upon you! to leave me in an island by myself, without the seed of Adam in it, and that I should not know this night what I shall do.'

He went forward about the island, and was seeing neither house nor tower in any place, low or high. At last he saw an old castle in the lower ground of the island, and he took his way towards it. He saw three youths coming heavily, wearily, tired to the castle. He spoke to them in instructed, eloquent, true, wise words of true wisdom. They spoke in return in like words.

They came in words of the olden time on each other; and who were here but his three true foster brothers. They went in right good pleasure of mind to the big town.

> They raised up music and laid down woe;
> There were soft drunken draughts
> And harsh, stammering drinks,
> Tranquil, easy toasts
> Between himself and his foster brethren,
> Music between fiddles, with which would sleep
> Wounded men and travailing women
> Withering away for ever; with the sound of that music
> Which was ever continuing sweetly that night.

They went to lie down. In the morning of the morrow he arose right well pleased, and he took his meat. What should he hear but the Gliogarsaich, clashing of arms and men going into their array. Who were these but his foster-brethren.

'Where are you going?' said he to them.

'We are from the end of a day and a year in this island,' said they, 'holding battle against MacDorcha MacDoilleir, the Son of Darkness Son of Dimness, and a hundred of his people, and every one we kill today they will be alive tomorrow. Spells are on us that we may not leave this for ever until we kill them.'

'I will go with you this day. You will be the better for me,' said he.

'Spells are on us,' said they, 'that no man may go with us unless he goes there alone.'

'Stay you within this day, and I will go there by myself,' said he.

He went away, and he hit upon the people of the Son of Darkness Son of Dimness, and he did not leave a head on a trunk of theirs.

He hit upon MacDorcha MacDoilleir himself, and MacDorcha

MacDoilleir said to him, 'Art thou here, Warrior of the Red Shield?'

'I am,' said the Warrior of the Red Shield.

'Well then,' said MacDorcha MacDoilleir, 'thou wilt not stand long for me.'

In each other's grips they went, and were hard belabouring each other till the mouth of dusk and lateness was. At last the Warrior of the Red Shield gave that cheery little light lift to the Son of Darkness Son of Dimness, and he put him under, and he cast the head off him.

Now there was MacDorcha MacDoilleir dead, and his thirteen sons, and the battle of a hundred on the hand of each one of them.

Then he was spoilt and torn so much that he could not leave the battlefield; and he did but let himself down, laid amongst the dead the length of the day. There was a great strand under him down below; and what should he hear but the sea coming as a blazing brand of fire, as a destroying serpent, as a bellowing bull. He looked from him, and what saw he coming on shore on the midst of the strand but a great toothy carlin, whose like was never seen. There was the tooth that was longer than a staff in her fist, and the one that was shorter than a stocking wire in her lap. She came up to the battlefield, and there were two between her and him. She put her finger in their mouths, and she brought them alive; and they rose up whole as best they ever were. She reached him and she put her finger in his mouth, and he snapped if off from the joint. She struck him a blow of the point of her foot, and she cast him over seven ridges.

'Thou pert little wretch,' said she, 'thou art the last I will next-live in the battlefield.'

The carlin went over another, and he was above her. He did not know how he should put an end to the carlin; he thought of throwing the short spear that her son had at her, and if the head should fall off her that was well. He threw the spear, and he drove the head off the carlin. Then he was stretched on the battlefield, blood and sinews and flesh in pain, but that he had whole bones. What should he see but a musical harper about the field.

Fairy dart (flint arrowhead), Scotland.

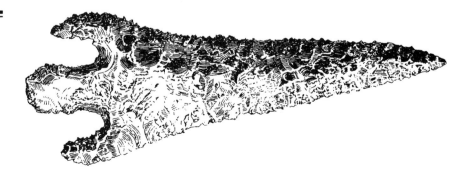

'What art thou seeking?' said he to the harper.

'I am sure thou art wearied,' said the harper. 'Come up and set thy head on this little hillock and sleep.'

He went up and he laid down. He drew a snore, pretending that he was asleep, and on his soles he was brisk, swift and active.

'Thou art dreaming,' said the harper.

'I am,' said he.

'What sawest thou?' said the harper.

'A musical harper,' he said, ' drawing a rusty old sword to take off my head.'

Then he seized the harper, and he drove the brain in fiery shivers through the back of his head.

Then he was under spells that he should not kill a musical harper for ever, but with his own harp.

Then he heard weeping about the field. 'Who is that?' said he.

'Here are thy three true foster-brothers, seeking thee from place to place today,' said they.

'I am stretched here,' said he, 'blood and sinews and bones in torture.'

'If we had the little vessel of balsam that the great carlin has, the mother of MacDorcha MacDoilleir, we would not be long in healing thee,' said they.

'She is dead herself up there,' said he, 'and she has nothing that ye may not get.'

'We are out of her spells for ever,' said they.

They brought down the little vessel of balsam, and they washed and bathed him with the thing that was in the vessel. Then he arose up as whole and healthy as he ever was. He went home with them, and they passed the night in great pleasure.

They went out the next day in great pleasure to play at shinty. He went against the three, and he would drive a half hail down, and a half hail up, in against them.

They perceived the Great Son of the Sons of the World coming to the town; that was their true foster-brother also. They went out where he was, and they said to him, 'Man of my love, avoid us and the town this day.'

'What is the cause?' said he.

'The Warrior of the Red Shield is within, and it is thou he is seeking,' said they.

'Go you home, and say to him to go away and to flee, or else that I will take the head off him,' said the Great Son of the Sons of the Universe.

Though this was in secret the Warrior of the Red Shield perceived it; and he went out on the other side of the house, and he struck a shield blow, and a fight kindling.

Kirk Michael cross,
Scotland.

The great warrior went out after him, and they began at each other.

There was no trick that is done by shield man or skiff man,
Or with cheater's dice box,
Or with organ of the monks,
That the heroes could not do;
As was the trick of Cleiteam, trick of Oigeam,
The apple of the juggler throwing it and catching it
Into each other's laps
Frightfully, furiously,
Bloodily, groaning, hurtfully.
Mind's desire! Umpire's choice!
They would drive three red sparks of fire from their armour,
Driving from the shield wall, and flesh
Of their breasts and tender bodies,
As they hardly belaboured each other.

'Art thou not silly, Warrior of the Red Shield, when thou art holding wrestling and had battle against me?' said Macabh Mhacaibh an Domhain.

'How is this?' said the hero of the Red Shield.

'It is that there is no warrior in the great world that will kill me till I am struck above the covering of the trews,' said Macabh Mor.

'The victory blessing of that be thine, telling it to me! If thou hadst told me that a long time ago, it is long since I had swept the head off thee,' said the Warrior of the Red Shield.

'There is in that more than thou canst do. The king's three teeth are in my pouch, and try if it be that thou will take them out,' said Macabh Mor.

When the Warrior of the Red Shield heard where the death of Macabh Mor was, he had two blows given for the blow, two thrusts for the thrust, two stabs for the stab; and the third was into the earth, till he had dug a hole; then he sprung backwards. The great warrior sprang towards him, and he did not notice the hole, and he went down into it to the covering of the trews. Then he reached him, and he cast off his head. He put his hand in his pouch, and he found the king's three teeth in it, and he took them with him and he reached the castle.

'Make a way for me for leaving this island,' said he to his foster-brethren, ' as soon as you can.'

'We have no way,' said they, 'by which thou canst leave it; but stay with us for ever, and thou shalt not want for meat or drink.'

'The matter shall not be so, but unless you make a way for letting me go, I will take the heads and necks out of you,' said he.

'A coracle that thy foster-mother and thy foster-father had is here, and we will send it with thee till thou goest on shore in Eirinn. The side that

The Sacrifice of Llew. The Flower Maiden, Bloduedd, contrives the ritual death of Llew Llaw Gyffes. This image is taken from 'Math son of Mathonwy', in the Welsh legends collected as *The Mabinogion*. (A version of this story is found in *Celtic Gods, Celtic Goddesses*, the companion volume to this book.) For another legend from *The Mabinogion*, see pages 15 – 24.

OVERLEAF LEFT: *Brigit*. The goddess Brigit, who represents the power of fire, light and transformation, is said in Celtic tradition to be foster-mother to the infant Jesus. This legend represents the movement from paganism to Celtic Christianity, with no antagonism between the two religions.

OVERLEAF RIGHT: *Branwen*. Branwen, imprisoned in Ireland, sends a starling with a message for her brother Bran.

thou settest her prow she will go with thee, and she will return back again by herself. Here are three pigeons for thee, and they will keep company with thee on the way,' said his foster-brothers to him.

He set the coracle out, and he sat in her, and he made no stop, no stay, till he went on shore in Eirinn. He turned her prow outwards, and if she was swift coming, she was swifter returning. He let away the three pigeons, as he left the strange country, and he was sorry that he had led them away, so beautiful was the music that they had.

There was a great river between him and the king's house. When he reached the river, he saw a hoary man coming with all his might, and shouting, 'Oh, gentleman, stay yonder until I take you over on my back, in case you should wet yourself.'

'Poor man, it seems as if thou wert a porter on the river,' said he.

'It is so,' said the hoary old man.

'And what set thee there?' said he.

'I will tell you that,' said the hoary old man. 'A big warrior struck a fist on the King of Erinn, and he drove out three of his teeth, and his two sons went to take out vengeance. There went with them a foolish little young boy that was son to me, and when they went to manhood, he went to faintness. It was but sorry vengeance for them to set me as porter on the river for it.'

'Poor man,' said he, 'that is no reproach. Before I leave the town thou wilt be well.'

He seized him, and he lifted him with him, and he set him sitting in the chair against the king's shoulder.

'Thou art but a saucy man that came to the town. Thou hast set that old carl sitting at my father's shoulder; and thou shalt not get it with thee,' said the Warrior of the Cairn, as he rose and seized him.

'By my hand, and by my two hands' redemption, it were as well for thee to seize Cnoc Leothaid as to seize me,' said the Warrior of the Red Shield to him, as he threw him down against the earth.

He laid on him the binding of the three smalls, straitly and painfully. He struck him a blow of the point of his foot, and he cast him over the seven highest spars that were in the court, under the drippings of the lamps, and under the feet of the big dogs; and he did the very same to the Warrior of the Sword; and the little treasure gave a laugh.

'Death wrappings be upon thyself!' said the king to her. 'Thou art from a year's end meat companion, and drink companion for me, and I never saw smile or laugh being made by thee, until my two sons are being disgraced.'

'Oh, king,' said she, 'I have knowledge of my own reason.'

'What, oh king, is the screeching and screaming that I am hearing since I came to the town? I never got time to ask till now,' said the hero of the Red Shield.

'My sons have three horses' teeth, driving them into my head, since the beginning of a year, with a hammer, until my head has gone through other with heartbreak and torment and pain,' said the king.

'What wouldst thou give to a man that would put thy own teeth into thy head, without hurt, without pain,' said he.

'Half my state so long as I may be alive, and my state altogether when I may go,' said the king.

He asked for a can of water, and he put the teeth into the water.

'Drink a draught,' said he to the king.

The king drank a draught, and his own teeth went into his head, firmly and strongly, quite as well as they ever were, and every one in her own place.

'Aha!' said the king, 'I am at rest. It is thou that didst the valiant deeds; and it was not my set of sons!'

'It is he,' said the little treasure to the king, 'that could do the valiant deeds; and it was not thy set of shambling sons, that would be stretched as seaweed seekers when he was gone to heroism.'

'I will not eat meat, and I will not drink draught,' said the king, 'until I see my two sons being burnt tomorrow. I will send some to seek faggots of grey oak for burning them.'

On the morning of the morrow, who was earliest on his knee at the king's bed but the Warrior of the Red Shield.

'Rise from that, warrior. What single thing mightest thou be asking that thou shouldst not get?' said the king.

'The thing I am asking is that thy two sons should be let go. I cannot be in any one place where I may see them spoiled,' said he. 'It were better to do bird and fool clipping to them, and to let them go.'

The king was pleased to do that. Bird and fool clipping was done to them. They were put out of their place, and dogs and big town vagabonds after them.

The little treasure and the Warrior of the Red Shield married, and agreed. A great wedding was made, that lasted a day and a year; and the last day of it was as good as the first day.

8

Merlin, Old and Young
(Wales)

MERLIN AND NIMUE

In this chapter we meet another famous (but often misrepresented) person from Celtic legend, the prophet Merlin. In the first story, which is my own invention from a traditional theme, the aged Merlin is under a strict obligation to find a sacred object. While fulfilling this obligation, he meets the Breton forest maiden Nimuë. Many variants of this tale are sexist and patriarchal, having the doting old man seduced by the wily young nymph. Here at last is the truth of the matter.

SOME tell that Merlin, with Taliesin the primary chief bard, took the wounded King Arthur to the Fortunate Isles. There the wise Morgen, skilled in all healing arts, watched over the Sleeping Lord, keeping him safe for the future. After they had sailed home, the prophet and the bard, what then? Taliesin founded an academy and spent his elder years teaching bards how to . . . well, how to do anything whatsoever, as he knew how to do everything and no one could take him anywhere or drink with him, so he might as well teach. But Merlin went again on his travels, remembering his days as a young man, a wild man, and a mad free man.

It was at about this time that a flock of wandering black birds came over from Ireland, calling themselves saints. These hairy vegetarians stumbled and strutted all over the land, and though some were steered hastily towards Europe, others founded cells and little centres of peace and love and rough wattle-and-daub hermitages in prime sites. Merlin

The Golden Ram Castle. The King of the Underworld guards the entrance to the castle of the Golden Ram Princess.

The Wasting Sickness of Cuchulainn. The hero Cuchulainn is scourged with whips by two fairy women.

OVERLEAF LEFT: *Old Merlin.* The aged Merlin waits deep in a rock for the right time to return. He carries with him the secret of Nimue.

OVERLEAF RIGHT: *Young Merlin.* The boy Merlin, with his mother, confronts the usurper Vortigern, and prepares to prophesy the future of the land.

was not filled with affection towards these Irish saints, for they took on the role of druids without knowledge of the law, the role of priests without knowing the Goddess, and the pose of prophets without knowing the power within the land. They preferred drab brown clothing and matted hair, and lived by begging and scrounging, abusing the sacred laws of hospitality. Even more absurdly, they ordered the tribes (who had been feuding since the age of bronze weapons) to love one another and show each other their cheeks, which was, of course, a powerful insult and provocation to war. And all this conflicting and confusing and misdirecting was supposed to originate with their sacrificed god, who was simply one of the many sacrificed gods who have passed to and fro since She gave birth to the Worlds.

No, Merlin did not like to see the Irish saints on the hilltops that had once been his, in the caves that had once been the home of bears, and most often upon the best river-valley sites that had been unused since Roman times. So he went to the great Caledonian forest, thinking that this could never be a prime site for development, and that the saintly gaggle and their flock would leave it unpecked. He was right, in part, and wrong too, for the first man that he met within the forest was a Culdee saint from Scotland. This one wore a woollen robe that was almost white, had his head shaved in a curious manner, and had washed only last week. He strode along with might and vigour, and in his right hand shook a bell without a clapper, which Merlin thought to be a special blessing.

'How I love the sound of that bell,' said Merlin, as he stooped to take a stone out from between his bare toes.

'Can a man love that which he does not know?' asked the Culdee saint, rhythmically pumping his bell up and down, and never a tinkle or clatter coming out of it.

'Indeed, I love it for itself, especially the unknown, unheard part of it, the mystery of its unringing and the discipline of your silently swinging of it to and fro, to and fro.'

'Do you not think it lacks something? Perhaps . . . the clapper?' asked the saint, marching along beside Merlin, even though he had been going in the opposite direction when they met. 'Perhaps a fine leaden clapper with a tiny cross cut deeply into it, or even a wooden clapper, though it might split, or one of granite with colours in the grain of it, or, God be praised, one of silver or of gold? Yes, gold would be good, the noble metal that gives tongue so sweetly.'

'I declare,' said Merlin, 'that the clapper which you have is perfect, the most perfect I have ever heard.'

'Ah, but the clapper of my bell is deep in the forest, far away,' replied the saint, deftly juggling the bell from hand to hand, 'hidden in the lair of the brown thief who took it from me.'

111

'Indeed,' Merlin murmured wisely, 'a sensitive bear or a delicate fox has been drawn by your immaculate spirituality to seek a relic of holiness to preserve for future ages.'

'No, it was a girl. A mere slip of a female girl,' and with this the Culdee crossed himself several times. 'She took it silently in the night, and in the bright morning I rang the bell three times before I realized that the clapper had been stolen.'

Merlin smiled a wise knowing learned mad inspired prophetic sad ecstatic half-smile, for the allusion was not lost upon him. In the bardic schools it was called a Taliesin slip, being a turn of phrase, unknowingly uttered, in which an everyday sexual forthrightness had hidden spiritual undertones. These undertones were detectable and interpreted only by a qualified bard, for the highest of fees.

'And now,' said Merlin to the saint, 'you ring your clapperless bell for your faith. I am astounded by your dedication to that which has been taken from you. Are you sure that you had it in the first place?' With these words he moved into the shadow of a stand of huge trees, ready to vanish before anything else could be said.

'Not so fast, grandad,' shouted the Culdee, grabbing the edge of the prophet's cloak. 'The bell is not clapperless, but absent from its clapper, for which the bell was made, for the clapper was in the world before it. And I ring it entirely and utterly to curse the thief. She called out of the wild rose bush, and put an obligation on the first creature who loved the silent bell, and only in this way can I get the clapper back.'

Merlin stopped, halfway between fight and flight, path and trackless wilderness, stone and thorn tree. He dared not move either way, for this sounded like a serious and obligatory obligation. 'I trust, learned saint, that you will find such a creature, but as for me I hate the sound of all bells, and have come this far to flee them. So, farewell . . .'

But the saint held fast to the cloak, whispering, 'You clearly said that you loved the silent bell, the earth and sky are my witnesses, the trees are my witnesses, and the stone that you removed from out of your toes. You cannot escape this obligation that I lay upon you: find the clapper that was in the world before the bell was. Bring it back to me by honest or devious ways. There is a blessing on those who serve.' By which he meant that there is a curse on those who do not.

And even as he whispered, the saint made the sign of the cross over Merlin, which no one had ever done before, and splashed him liberally with strong distilled spirits from a little flask that was hanging around his neck. Merlin flinched, licked his lips, and so was utterly trapped by the obligation laid upon him.

As he plunged wildly through the thorn bushes, cloak torn, arms flapping like a crow, eyes goggling in opposite directions, Merlin thought he heard the Culdee laugh a deep belly-laugh, not like that of a Christian

Tam Lin. Tam Lin undergoes a series of shape-changes as his lover Janet liberates him from the power of the Queen of Fairy.

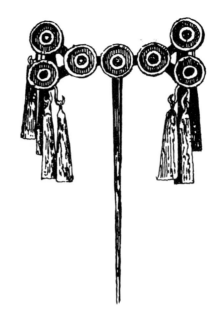

saint but like a hero or even a god after a great feast. His last coherent thought as he plunged into darkness was, I thought I'd stopped doing this kind of thing years ago.

While Merlin was plunging, a young woman was bathing in a shallow forest pool. First she unbound her black curling hair, letting it fall to her waist. From out of this mass of hair flowing and twining in all directions she took a number of curious objects. A garland of red and white briar roses came first, which had held her hair up. Next, from the depth of the thick curls, she pulled out a tiny golden pin in the shape of a wren. After that a small roll of parchment, tied with a red ribbon, a roll small enough and tight enough to be carried by a starling for as long a distance as there is sea between Ireland and Wales. Last, from the deepest, blackest depths of that thicket of dark hair, she teased out a dark stone, rubbed and rounded into the shape of a tiny pregnant body, with bulging breasts and thighs. This image she placed revertently in the centre of the briar rose garland, to keep it safe from all directions. But the golden wren and the flying scroll she hung by coloured threads upon a branch, where the four winds could turn them as they willed, pivoting each around its unique centre.

Now she lifted her arms and pulled off her ragged shift. Her body was strong and brown, and only slightly moss-green and muddy from splashing through the little streams and over logs and in and out of the marshes and hollows filled with dead leaves and rain. She had built a conical fire stacked with juniper berries and herbs, and into the smoke of this she hung her shift, upon a three-forked staff thrust firmly into the damp earth. Thus naked, her breasts uplifting with the cold air, she jumped into the pool. The pool was not deep, and she was not tall, so she settled happily with the icy water up to her nose, sitting upon the bright sand where the spring bubbled forth, and whispering her blessing through dark lips barely above the light surface. She sighed and settled further, and as her hair floated out over the surface in coils and snakes and spirals and weavings, Merlin fell out of the tangled trees and into the pool.

What happened next? What happened next . . . I hear you say. What *unhappened* was this, though the telling of it is not as strange and true as the unhappening of it. The clouds stopped moving, the sun blinked, the four winds of the world drew a quick breath inwards, and all the animals and birds and fish that were in contact with the earth lifted their feet or bellies or fins entirely off the branches or stones or sand or ground or wherever they were positioned. Fires stood still and ceased to dance, waters paused in their flowing, and all falling things remained in one place, even in mid-fall. Far away in the forest someone stopped ringing a clapperless bell for an instant and closed his eyes tight and screwed up his face in anticipation. And all this for the merest fraction of the delusion of time that it takes for a grey-haired wild-eyed madman to fall out of a thorny thicket and get a poke in the eye with a firm young nipple. Otherwise, everything remained the same.

'Unusually dry weather for the time of year,' said Merlin casually.

'Yes,' she agreed, moving the merest fraction out of politeness, 'only four full days of rain this week.'

'And then there were the two and a half half-days of rain.'

'Out of the seven, five and quarter of rain is good.'

'Indeed, unusually good and dry.'

Having observed the rules of politeness, the girl stood up and stepped out of the pool and over to her scented smoky fire. Merlin made himself more comfortable in the freezing water, wriggling down on to the sand and little stones, feeling them press on his thighs. One eye looked up at the cloudy sky through the treetops, while the other looked without blinking at the girl.

'Might one be allowed to ask,' he murmured in Greek, 'what might be the name of a young woman who lives in the forest, bathes in pools and wears rose garlands in her hair?'

'One might be allowed to ask,' she answered in Pictish, 'but might not obtain an answer unless the question was phrased correctly. For example – and here she showed her youthful impetuosity by switching to local Welsh – 'if she were asked if her name was Gwladys, the answer would be no. If Einid, also no. If Branwen, then not exactly.'

'Aha,' said Merlin in Latin. 'But such a girl, assuming that she existed in the first place, might have a connection, however tenuous, with Branwen, daughter of Llyr?'

'She might,' said the girl in Irish. Merlin swivelled his eyes without moving his head, until one looked at the girl, and the other looked at the tree with the objects hanging from it by red and black threads, moving slowly in the forest winds.

'And if that connection was a tiny scroll,' he murmured in Breton, which was close to Welsh so perhaps he was being lazy, 'would that tiny scroll, between heaven and earth as it is, contain this girl's true name?'

'No, it would not,' she snapped in perfect hieratic Egyptian, 'for her true name is not to be written down in any form of letters, signs or words.'

Merlin blinked, first one eye, then the other. He knew now that her native language was Breton Welsh, and that she had a Pictish mother. The priestesses' tongue of Egypt troubled him slightly, for it was no longer spoken in that land, though one could learn it in the normal way in dreams and visions. He knew also that she honoured the Mother, and that she carried the vengeance of Branwen against all men within her heart. He was sure, though he had no proof, that she was the thief of the clapper. He sighed and waited for her to say something more. While he waited, he inwardly recited an epic tale that can take up to four days in the telling, and marvelled at his own impatience in choosing such a short one.

'I propose an exchange,' she said in Saxon, which caused Merlin to fall over into the water. He would have spat at the sound of it, but for his respect for the spirit of the pool.

'Yet you insult me by the language you use to suggest it,' he said, attempting to focus both eyes upon her at once. This he could do only by wagging his head from side to side.

'No insult was intended; I merely had to be sure that you were listening properly.' She had reverted to Welsh, and they both continued to talk in the blessed angelic tongue.

'I propose an exchange thus: you wish to know a maiden's name and I wish to keep it secret. You discover how I may keep my name secret and I will tell it to you.'

Merlin did not pause to think, but spoke with the tongue, the inspired speech, that comes upon prophets and madmen instantly and may not be denied. 'Send your name through time, so that it is not found either in the past or in the present, but will be found in the future when the world is ready for it.'

'Indeed, indeed, just as the Sleeping Lord is waiting in time to return from the Fortunate Isles. And a shame that is, for I have the only thing will heal him.'

Merlin gasped and goggled and could hardly breathe. He leapt out of the pool and sloshed his way over to the fire, reaching out for her.

'What is it? Where is it?' he croaked, forgetting all the rules of the game. But she slipped out of his cold, wet hands, and plunged into her dress, hanging as it was from the three-pronged staff. She snatched up the little black stone figurine, and waved it over her head, then held it close to her breasts.

'It is this image of the Mother, from the dawn of time, when our ancestors walked as equals with the people of the *sidh* and as companions with the birds and beasts and fish. And without this no wounded man can be cured, even if he be the king himself. And I reclaimed it from a thief, who had taken it to be the clapper of a bell.'

Merlin sat down for a moment upon the fire of scented twigs and berries, then leapt up again with his robe and cloak smoking and steaming at the same time. This was the very object that he was obliged to retrieve, yet it surely did not belong in the saintly bell. It was the very object that he had to retrieve, yet he himself needed it for the healing of the king, which meant the healing of the land through time. He could neither meet the obligation nor cheat it. Whatever he did would be wrong.

'I will make this bargain with you,' he said, and his eyes came into full focus as his clarity of mind returned. 'I will take your name through time with me, and promise to guard it. In return you will give me the Mother stone, and in return for that I will take it too, with your name, through time, where no saints shall steal it, and where it will be hidden, ready to come to the Sleeping Lord when it is time for him to awaken.'

Bronze ornament with triple-snake pattern.

'Done,' she said, and with complete trust handed him the little black stone figure of the Goddess from the dawn of time, when all beings in the world were equal and walked together in joy and peace. Merlin blinked for an instant, for as he took the figure in his hands, a flurry of images seemed to blow like leaves past his eyes. The last one was of a huge red-haired man with stag's antlers upon his head, wearing a flaming cloak all fire within and green leaves without, spinning around and around, and turning himself into the image of Christian saint, laughing all the while.

Merlin nodded at this, and walked around the clearing, around the pool three times. On his third circuit, he came to something that he had not seen on the first two, though surely it had been there all the while. It was a great rock, seamed with white quartz, greater than the size of a man. He laid his forehead against, then one ear, listening. He put the little Goddess into one of the many pockets in his robe and cast off his cloak. Then, leaning into the rock, he passed his hands over it, and it quivered.

'This will do,' he said, and passed his hands through it. When his arms were deep in the stone, up to the shoulders, and half of his face was gone in, and his knees, and feet, she came over and stood close to him. Then he was in the stone completely, and merged with it, and no one passing by would know he was there, except that they might see the shape of an old man in the folds and shadows of the rock. Then she pressed her dark lips to where his ear might be in the rock, and her warm, moist breath passed into it, as she whispered, 'My name is Nimuë.'

THE BOY MERLIN

With this legend, we turn to one of the earliest literary sources for Celtic myths and legends from Wales, the twelfth-century writings of Geoffrey of Monmouth. Most of the significant characteristics of the Celtic Merlin are not those of the wise old man but those of the boy or foolish young man. These themes are well represented, from bardic (originally druidic) tradition, in the works of Geoffrey.

Here, in a passage from his *History of the Kings of Britain*, he has the boy Merlin confronting the usurper King Vortigern and confounding the false soothsayers with his insights. In another scene, not quoted here, the boy Merlin utters the 'Prophecies', a substantial set of predictions and apocalyptic visions that reach into the twenty-first century.

Book V, Chapter XVII

aT last he had recourse to magicians for their advice, and commanded them to tell him what course to take. They advised him to build a very strong tower for his own safety, since he had lost all his other fortified places. Accordingly he made a progress about the country, to find out a convenient situation, and came at last to Mount Erir, where he assembled workmen from several countries, and ordered them to build the tower. The builders, therefore, began to lay the foundation; but whatever they did one day the earth swallowed up the next, so as to leave no appearance of their work. Vortigern being informed of this again consulted with his magicians concerning the cause of it, who told him that he must find out a youth that never had a father, and kill him, and then sprinkle the stones and cement with his blood; for by those means, they said, he would have a firm foundation. Hereupon messengers were dispatched away over all the provinces, to enquire out such a man. In their travels they came to a city, called afterwards Kaermerdin, where they saw some young men, playing before the gate, and went up to them; but being weary with their journey, they sat down in the ring, to see if they could meet with what they were in quest of. Towards evening, there happened on a sudden a quarrel between two of the young men, whose names were Merlin and Dabutius. In the dispute Dabutius said to Merlin: 'You fool, do you presume to quarrel with me? Is there any equality in our birth? I am descended of royal race, both by my father and mother's side. As for you, nobody knows what you are, for you never had a father.' At that word the messengers looked earnestly upon Merlin, and asked the bystanders who he was. They told him, it was not known who was his father; but that his mother was daughter to the king of Dimetia, and that she lived in St Peter's church among the nuns of that city.

Chapter XVIII

Vortigen enquires of Merlin's mother concerning her conception of him.

Upon this the messengers hastened to the governor of the city, and ordered him, in the king's name, to send Merlin and his mother to the king. As soon as the governor understood the occasion of their message, he readily obeyed the order, and sent them to Vortigern to complete his design. When they were introduced into the king's presence, he received the mother in a very respectful manner, on account of her noble birth; and began to enquire of her by what man she had conceived. 'My sovereign lord,' said she, 'by the life of your soul and mine, I know nobody that begot him of me. Only this I know, that as I was once with my

companions in our chambers, there appeared to me a person in the shape of a most beautiful young man, who often embraced me eagerly in his arms, and kissed me; and when he had stayed a little time, he suddenly vanished out of my sight. But many times after this he would talk with me when I sat alone, without making any visible appearance. When he had a long time haunted me in this manner, he at last lay with me several times in the shape of a man, and left me with child. And I do affirm to you, my sovereign lord, that excepting that young man, I know nobody that begot him of me.' The king, full of admiration at this account, ordered Maugantius to be called, that he might satisfy him as to the possibility of what the woman had related. Maugantius, being introduced, and having the whole matter repeated to him, said to Vortigern: 'In the books of our philosophers, and in a great many histories, I have found that several men have had the like original. For, as Apuleius informs us in his book concerning the Demon of Socrates, between the moon and the earth inhabit those spirits, which we will call incubuses. These are of the nature partly of men and partly of angels, and whenever they please they assume human shapes and lie with women. Perhaps one of them appeared to this woman, and begot that young man of her.'

Chapter XIX

Merlin's speech to the king's magicians, and advice about the building of the tower.

Merlin in the meantime was attentive to all that had passed, and then approached the king, and said to him, 'For what reason am I and my mother introduced into your presence?'

'My magicians,' answered Vortigern, 'advised me to seek out a man that had no father, with whose blood my building is to be sprinkled, in order to make it stand.'

'Order your magicians,' said Merlin, 'to come before me, and I will convict them of a lie.'

The king was surprised at his words, and presently ordered the magicians to come, and sit down before Merlin, who spoke to them after this manner: 'Because you are ignorant what it is that hinders the foundation of the tower, you have recommended the shedding of my blood for cement to it, as if that would presently make it stand. But tell me now, what is there under the foundation? For something there is that will not suffer it to stand.'

The magicians at this began to be afraid, and made him no answer.

Then said Merlin, who was also called Ambrose, 'I entreat your majesty would command your workmen to dig into the ground, and you will find a pond which causes the foundation to sink.'

This accordingly was done, and presently they found a pond deep under ground, which had made it give way. Merlin after this went again to the magicians and said, 'Tell me, ye false sycophants, what is there under the pond.' But they were silent. Then said he again to the king, ' Command the pond to be drained, and at the bottom you will see two hollow stones, and in them two dragons asleep.' The king made no scruple of believing him, since he had found true what he said of the pond, and therefore ordered it to be drained: which done, he found as Merlin had said; and now was possessed with the greatest admiration of him. Nor were the rest that were present less amazed at his wisdom, thinking it to be no less than divine inspiration.

(trans. J. A.Giles, 1896)

Accordingly, while Vortigern, King of the Britons, was yet seated upon the bank of the pool that had been drained, forth issued the two dragons, whereof the one was white and the other red. And when the one had drawn anigh unto the other, they grappled together in baleful combat and breathed forth fire as they panted. But presently the white dragon did prevail, and drove the red dragon unto the verge of the lake. But he, grieving to be thus driven forth, fell fiercely again upon the white one, and forced him to draw back. And whilst that they were fighting on this wise, the King bade Ambrosius Merlin declare what this battle of the dragons did portend.

(trans. S.Evans, 1912)

Book VIII, Chapter I

Merlin, by delivering these and many other prophecies, caused in all that were present an admiration at the ambiguity of his expressions. But Vortigern above all the rest both admired and applauded the wisdom and prophetical spirits of the young man; for that age had produced none that ever talked in such a manner before him. Being therefore curious to learn his own fate, he desired the young man to tell him what he knew concerning that particular. Merlin answered: 'Fly the fire of the sons of Constantine, if you are able to do it: already are they fitting out their ships: already are they leaving the Armorican shore: already are they spreading out their sails to the wind. They will steer towards Britain: they will invade the Saxon nation: they will subdue that wicked people; but they will first burn you, being shut up in a tower. To your own ruin did you prove a traitor to their father, and invite the Saxons into the island. You invited them for your safeguard; but they came for a punishment to you. Two deaths instantly threaten you; nor is it easy to determine which you can best avoid. For on the one hand the Saxons

shall lay waste your country, and endeavour to kill you; on the other shall arrive the two brothers, Aurelius Ambrosius and Uther Pendragon, whose business will be to revenge their father's murder upon you. Seek out some refuge if you can: tomorrow they will be on the shore of Totness. The faces of the Saxons shall look red with blood, Hengist shall be killed, and Aurelius Ambrosius shall be crowned. He shall bring peace to the nation: he shall restore the churches; but shall die of poison. His brother Uther Pendragon shall succeed him, whose days also shall be cut short by poison. There shall be present at the commission of this treason your own issue, whom the boar of Cornwall shall devour.'
Accordingly the next day early arrived Aurelius Ambrosius and his brother, with ten thousand men.

(trans. J.A. Giles, 1896)

Bronze breast-pinss.

tam lin, or the game of Chess
(Scotland)

9

In 'The Wooing of Etain' (Chapter 2) and 'The Wasting Sickness of Cuchulainn' (Chapter 5) we find the theme of love between the realms and races, human and fairy. This legend takes many forms, and in 'The Game of Chess' a human woman seeks to draw her human lover back from the fairy realm. This is my own version of a classic Scottish ballad that contains a wealth of pagan and fairy lore.

The traditional, magical ballad 'Tam Lin' forms the basis for this tale. Long and complex variations of the ballad exist, known to singers in Scotland and America and there are several European parallels.

'Tam Lin' has a multi-faceted theme, or a knot of themes, that cannot be fully undone or cut through. It seems, initially, to relate to fairy traditions, in which a human is captured by the Queen of Fairy and his true love releases him by a ritual at the crossroads. This meaning, however, is possibly the last or uppermost of many levels, reaching far back into ancient myth and ritual. Rather than attempt yet another analysis of the ballad, I have chosen to focus upon a retelling of the tale.

As is often the case, certain apparently minor elements leap forward demanding attention, mainly 'The Game of Chess'. In the original narrative, four and twenty ladies gay are playing at the chess, and in comes the fair young Janet, as pale as any glass. What was a poetic device, perhaps, suddenly becomes a major focus for the tale. Furthermore, when Janet retrieves Tam Lin from the grasp of the Otherworld, she also puts an end to the game. It is not, however, chess as we know it in this world today.

As in the original ballad, it is not clear in this story whether Janet is rescuing her lover or actually giving birth to him as a child; the sequence of mysterious lover, pregnancy and magical birth is found in most myths and religions, and need not be elaborated here.

Modern interpretations of the traditional tale of Tam Lin have dwelt at great length upon his sequence of transformations, likening them, rightly, to alchemical changes, to the seasons and months of the years, and to the shamanistic or magical changes undertaken by initiates in the the old primal Mysteries. Personally, I do not think that there is a 'complete' or 'correct' sequence of transformations: there are different transformations for each individual, though most changes partake of a general sequence rooted in the interaction between humanity and the environment, represented by many myths, legends and specific magical practices. In this story, therefore, the changes undergone by Tam Lin are, intentionally, not clearly defined, though they do seem to connect with the mysteries of gestation and childbirth.

The vessels for water and milk which stand at the crossroads are derived from actual ritual vessels, long preserved at many sites. Few of these remain today, though examples may be found at prehistoric sites in Ireland. In the nineteenth century, local people told Sir Walter Scott (though his testimony must always be taken with a certain amount of caution, as he fabricated a great deal to suit himself) that the fairy-rings found in his locality were the actual site of Janet's ritual reclamation of Tam Lin into the human world. Whatever the validity of this, we do know that fairy-rings, or zones of rich growth, are found at certain ancient sites; in Scotland, offerings of fresh milk were poured regularly upon such spots as tokens of regard or perhaps propitiation to the fairy folk. Little wonder, a cynic might say, that the grass grows so greenly upon such sites, with such a tradition of enrichment of the soil.

The Fairy Queen in this tale is not a glittering little sprite with a shining wand; she is, in fact, the Great Queen or Phantom Queen, Morrighan, a terrifying goddess of the pagan Celts, acknowledged even by materialist psychology as a dark constituent of our consciousness. General literature on Western spiritual and magical traditions has tended to lose sight of such potent female figures, though they are well preserved in Eastern traditions to this day, and have always played a major role in the practical, magical and mystical arts of the West.

Yet the Dark Goddess is, despite long efforts to purge her from the imagination, well known in early literature, legend, myth and inscription in the West and her suppression is, of course, a matter of Christian history. Her revival, however, is not a matter of cosy pseudo-paganism. She is a potent, demolishing and empowering force in nature and within ourselves; no true spiritual development or magical initiation may occur without her double-edged blessing.

She appears in tradition, and in this tale in triple form, though not necessarily in the well-publicized triplications found in modern literature. In 'Tam Lin' certain well-described images are used for the Fairy Queen, who appears, or rather utters curses without actually being seen in person, towards the close of the ballad. Three of these, allocated to three of the Four Directions, are found in this tale. They are, in short, key images of the Great Goddess in her dark or destructive aspect: black crows flying over white ice; a flowering broom plant (*Sarothamnus scoparius*) within a cloud of fire; and the cry of an owl within which is the voice of a young girl. Needless to say, these are not images to be worked with lightly or superficially; the imaginative forces aroused by this sequence may be balanced according to the Four Directions, just as they are in the dramatization of the story itself.

Í T was the chess tournament: twenty-four women, in twelve games, playing against one another. The winner of each game would progress about the great square gold and greenstone table, being herself a transforming game piece in a pattern. The final role, of course, was that of Queen. Each square of the table was in itself a board, either green inlaid with alternate silver squares, or gold inlaid with alternate black squares. The inner boards were played by using long, finely carved ivory wands to move each piece, though skilled players could move their pieces by other means.

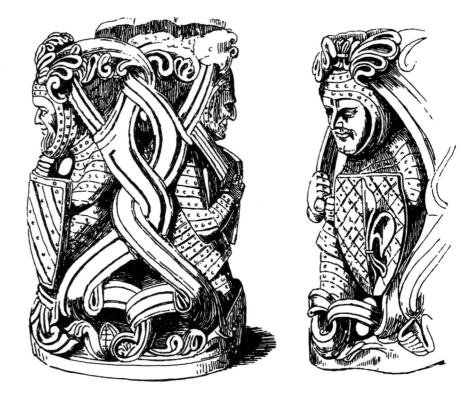

Medival chess-pieces from the Scottish Antiquarian Museum (nineteenth-century collection). Chess in various forms was a magical or cosmological game in the ancient world.

Kirk Bradden Cross, Scotland.

Janet leaned over the cold stone balustrade and looked down upon the game below, six women to each of the four sides of the huge game table, and the squares flashing brilliant colours in the morning sunlight. She felt sick, as she had for several mornings past. Each crystalline chess-man uttered a fine ringing sound as it was touched by the wand of a player, and a constant flow of assonant tones filled the great room, echoing back from the domed ceiling far above. The high, clear tones and the flashing colours made her even more nauseous, and she was glad that she had not been selected to play this year, even though her playing would have been a courtesy matter only, she being the high king's daughter.

As she stepped back from the balustrade, about to return to her chamber and wait for the nausea to pass, she felt a deep pulling sensation within her. It was as if some innermost part of her body was being drawn away, and must drag the rest with it, or be torn out. She knew that upon the hill someone was blowing a horn, and felt in her deep dress pocket for the withered rose. A thorn stabbed into her thumb and drew blood, and as she sucked the blood away to ease her pain, the pulling started again.

Upon the great game table below, pieces began to vibrate suddenly, causing the players to look about in alarm. Clearly the distant horn was reaching even the crystal pieces: the men at arms, warriors, maidens, the deadman, and the queen, upon each board. Janet withdrew quickly before she could be seen.

From her room a small stone stair led down into a back courtyard, and through the courtyard door she darted, out into open country beyond. It was not a long walk to the little wood upon the hill which her father had given to her, but before she reached the outermost trees, the silent horn blew again, tearing at her innards. She ran into the low thorny bushes, the wild roses that had been her special gift, and on under the hazel trees. Towards the centre of the wood was a bubbling spring, where, she knew, someone awaited her.

Pausing, panting for breath, she leaned against a hawthorn tree close to the clear pool. He was here, she was certain, but could not be seen. Three times he had blown his horn to summon her, yet was further off now than he had ever been.

When they had first met he had appeared suddenly beside her, a solid handsome man, with dark curling hair and deep brown eyes. She had plucked her first rose of the spring that day, rejoicing that her father had given her this rose- and hazel-wood as her own special place, perhaps with some good magic in it. But with her tearing of rose from branch, the young man had stepped out of the bushes suddenly, with no sound of rustling branches or snapping twigs. He had been angry too, demanding by what right she pulled flowers for her hat in this hallowed place. But she had laughed, and told him that her father owned all the

126

land around, and had given her the little hill for her very own wild pleasure garden.

What had happened next was a mystery, for the handsome young man seemed to blur and shimmer, dissolving into a golden cloud, humming like bees upon a hot summer day; while she herself felt drowsy yet seething with insatiable savage desire. When she woke she was in her own bed at home, with the pleasant morning light shining through the long tapestry that hung over the deep window. She thought it had all been a dream. Until the morning sickness.

So she had gone to the wood again, to find that small grey herb which old women talked about in whispers, and again the man had appeared, or rather his voice had come to her out of a thick tangled mass of wild roses, woodbine and hazel. This time he had told her his name, Tam Lin, and that he was guardian of the wood, set to watch the spring and the rose bushes by the queen of the land. Janet had not believed this, for her own father ruled hereabouts, but in the confusion of his voice from the bushes, and the sudden warmth that she felt for him, even though he remained unseen, she forgot to pull the abortificant.

And now he had summoned her with a terrible unrelenting summons, drawing upon the child in her womb by some means that she could not understand. At the centre of the wood, by the clear pool, she waited for him to speak. This time his voice was very faint, as if travelling a great distance, yet it was right by her ear, as if he also stood beside her and whispered gently.

Now he told her that he was a prisoner of the Great Queen, and that she and her terrible people intended to sacrifice him at the November feast, when the gates between the living and the dead stood open for a brief wild moment. Janet pitied him then, and pitying him she remembered that she loved him, as if it was something that she had always known but had superficially forgotten while busy with the trivia of her entire life to this very moment in time and space.

Three times she had met him, and each time he had been further from her. Three times he had blown his horn to summon her and now he was furthest away, yet closer and clearer than ever. She listened well to the instructions that he offered, and when his voice finally faded, and only the sounds of the wood could be heard through the rising wind, she quietly went home to wait for the festival in November.

But by that time, of course, her belly was swelling, and her father had long since found her out, and challenged her to name her lover. Her obstinate refusal enraged him, and he swore that she would be married to whatever half-decent warrior or chieftain might have her, bastard and all. After all, she was a high king's daughter, as much as anyone could tell, and he could sweeten her pregnancy with many gifts.

Janet refused to consider such an outrageous idea, and no matter how much her father shouted and raged, disturbing the chess players below the gallery where he and she stood jut-chinned and hands on hips arguing, she refused to be married. It was her right to choose her own husband, just as it was her blood that carried the royal lineage, and not his. Such pretensions from a man, father, king!

The king pulled his plaited, silk-ribboned, orange beard, and slapped himself in the face several times, turning purple with rage. Then he stamped off to muck out the pigsty, which was, of course, the royal prerogative. The chess game settled down again, and one tall, calm lady moved her queen with an elaborate flourish of her fingers. The piece glided swiftly across the central board to check-mate the deadman. The adjudicators beat upon their huge bronze gongs until the royal hall vibrated in every stone. Dust swept out of tiny cracks in the roof, abandoned game pieces fell over on their boards, and as the reverbation died, nobody dared tell the king that he was about to be married again. But, of course, the pigs had already told him, and it did not improve his temper in the slightest.

The November festival came not long after the royal marriage that year, so many of the wedding games ran on into those for the turning of the winter stars. But no one could hide the tension as the turning time approached: there were many dead friends, relatives, enemies, to consider, and always there were unspoken questions about the year to come.

So in the very centre pit of night, when beans had been cast, fires raked through, milk poured, and much wine and beer drunk, everyone lay snoring or trembling in their sleeping chambers or on the rushes upon the chess-hall floor. Janet, however, was wide awake, and creeping towards the back courtyard gate.

She carried, with difficulty, a great skin bag full of fresh milk, which she herself had taken from the huge vat of that day's milking, declaring that she wanted it to bathe in. It was heavy, and made loud gurgling and deep slapping sounds, as if to announce itself to all and sundry whenever she passed. She had never realized that milk was so noisy.

Beyond the gate she had tethered a quiet donkey, who patiently allowed her to sling the grumbling milk across its back, and walked by her side towards the dark wood upon the distant hill.

The night was very still indeed, as if all sounds had been terminated. The stars were small and clear. On this night the terrible armies and hosts of the Otherworld were said to ride, yet all was peaceful. Janet felt suddenly cheated by the silence, and then relief replaced her fear. Perhaps nothing bad would happen at all, she thought to herself.

As Janet, the donkey and the grumbling milk crept through the dark meadow towards the trees, they felt a deep vibration in the damp earth beneath. It was as if a host of riders passed through the ground far below

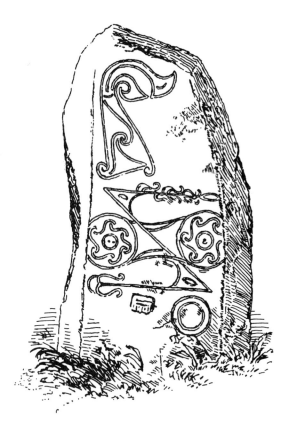

Dunnichen Stone, showing
Pictish symbols, Scotland.

them, the hoofs muffled by the clay, yet distinct enough to recognize
even individual horses. But within a few moments the sound had
dwindled into the distance. Janet increased her pace, so the donkey
added its complaint in concert with the milk. They reached the border
of the wood, where the first few stunted bushes reached out of blackest
shadows, but instead of striking into the trees, she took a faint path
around the woodland, towards the high crossroads beyond. Again she
felt the host pass through the earth beneath her, the sounds were louder
now, as if they neared the surface, and even a faint sound of voices could
be heard, crying in a high strange language.

Now the donkey brayed and tried to bolt. She coaxed his ears with
tickling and breathing, and he plodded on, leaving the woodland behind,
and coming out on to the high bones of the downland. As they moved
so slowly through the cold night towards the open crossroads, Janet
realized that the rumbling beneath the earth had first travelled from
behind her and then from her right. It was as if the unseen host of riders
had travelled south to north, and then east to west. She could not
understand this at all, and used the puzzle to suppress her growing fear.
There was no logical answer to this problem, she decided, and, seeking
further distraction from terror, she listened instead to the milk. It seemed
to be saying:

First I was green,
But now I am white,
First I was warm
Now I freeze in the night . . .

This gloomy message helped her not at all. She laid her hands upon the great leather bag, and it drew the warmth out of them. Deep inside her, her baby suddenly kicked, then became still.

Four ancient upland roads met together at a high, flat place, and there Janet, donkey, milk and baby stopped. She quickly lowered the bag of milk from the donkey's back, and he stood trembling with fear. At the very centre of the crossroads a tall menhir rose up towards the stars, and upon it a thoughtful missionary had carved the figure of a small man with a teardrop-shaped head, his arms spread out wide in the shape of a cross. She doubted very much if this religious emblem would protect her, but gently touched it out of respect for all victims upon the Wheel, no matter what name or origin. As she did so, a faint flow of energy seemed to emanate from the figure, as if it moved slightly beneath the warmth of her touch. Again the baby in her womb kicked, then settled peacefully.

The milk had stopped complaining as soon as it was set upon the ground, and Janet looked about her for the stone basins. There they were, overgrown with long grass, unused for many years. Two deeply etched bowls, each big enough to hold a human. In the cold, under the faintest starlight, she pulled the grasses away, and scraped the bowls clean, using a bundle of long grass and ferns to make a thorough job of it. She could feel the spiral patterns in the stone, but could hardly see them. Into one bowl she poured the milk, which made such a loud noise as it poured that the donkey bolted off into the dark, his small hooves tapping lightly, speedily, upon the stones of the road.

Now she felt the need for haste, for the middle of the night must be drawing near. Using the empty skin, she drew water from the traveller's well at the foot of the menhir, and filled the second basin. As the water reached the brim, dark clouds seethed overhead, and suddenly she could see nothing. In the distance, coming it seemed down all four roads, and upon the very surface of the earth, she could hear a host of riders. The bridle bells rang, shrill bird-like voices called and cried, harnesses jingled and the ground began to shake at their coming.

Then four great hosts, one from each corner of the land, drew near to the crossroads, and in the total darkness Janet knew that she would fail, for she could see nothing. Cowering behind the tall stone, she realized that she could not tell any difference between the black, brown and white horses as her lover had bidden her. He would be riding on the milk-white steed, after the first black and the first brown horse to reach the crossroads. But all horses are black in the dark.

The host surrounded her with a great roaring and pounding and ringing. She heard their long lance-heads clashing and for the first time smelt the heady perfume of their kind, making her head spin and wild sensations flow through her body. Then she felt again that terrible pull from within. So strongly it came that she was jerked out of hiding in the shadow beneath the stone like a helpless puppet, her muscles working despite her will. The blackness was lit by flashes of white and green and gold, shimmering outlines of wild figures with long flowing hair and violet eyes; a wildfire flowed over and around and through the great host that milled and merged about the cross, seeking a new direction for their charge. And the white horse shone like a star, like a mirror reflecting the dawn, like love within a maiden's eyes as she lies with her first man. Upon it he rode, with a tall, spiralling, crystal crown upon his head and blank unseeing eyes. Just as he had bidden, in full defiance of the host, she leapt upon him and dragged him to the ground.

Instantly the riders formed a great circle about her, galloping and screaming, forming a blur of colours and sound. She lay panting upon the still form of the man, seeing the shards of the crown glitter upon the rough stones all about. Then she felt his shape begin to change.

His body elongated beneath her, his hair lengthened and coarsened and the rank smell of a wild beast came from him. Rippling muscles sought to shake her off and a gust of hot, meat-rotten air roared out of his fanged lion's mouth. But she held on to him gently, as if the vicious beast raging beneath was her own baby, and suddenly the lion shape sagged and melted. The host fell silent, circling her with a hissing of indrawn breath, faster and faster yet, until the ground trembled only slightly, as if they passed above it in their spinning. She did not lift her eyes off the ground, knowing that she must not yet look at whatever she held, nor at the circling riders.

But as the riders gained speed, so did the transformations. She felt an amorphous sea beast, a lithe dry serpent, a clicking hook-jawed insect that rasped its legs against her face, tearing her skin, a flapping bird with a harsh beak and claws; other shapes and smells and sensations followed one after another, each trying its uttermost to throw her off and away from out of the shadow of the protecting stone, out under the hoofs of the circling host.

Then the transformations paused, and she felt heat. Her eyes were tightly closed; she felt the shape beneath her become rigid like metal. Hot metal; the burning calor of it seared her hands, singed her eyebrows away, and she could smell the burning of flesh and hair. With a great burst of strength, she flung the burning metal into the bowl of well water, and a cloud of steam shot up high into the night.

The circling host stopped dead, horses staggering into one another and spear-heads clashed and tangled. Still the water seethed and boiled as something struggled within the ancient basin to gain shape. The stone seemed to glow with heat, and in that dim light she saw what might be a hand, glowing amber with flickering blue veins and red bones showing clearly through it. She crawled to the basin, and pulled herself upright, defiantly gazing upon the vast multitide that watched now in stillness and silence. Reaching in, she lifted the glowing man-shape firmly, grasping it beneath each armpit, and with a scream threw it over into the basin of fresh milk. Instantly the milk began to talk; it babbled with voices that she knew, her mother and her mother's mother, both dead, her long-buried aunts, her murdered sisters, all entreating her to take this terrible man-shape away before it destroyed them and cast them into the shadows with its golden heat. Then the milk slowly turned blood-red, first in streaks, then in broad clots, then into widening veins. As it turned to blood it fell silent, but the man-shape within beat its arms and legs, thrashing about until it fell out on to the grass. A beautiful naked man, unconscious. She wrapped her long green mantle about him, cradling him in her arms, wrapping him until not one part of him from head to toe could be seen.

The clouds above rolled back as if a great wind had snatched at them, and the cold clear light of a full moon shone into the circle. Suddenly she was aware of the army surrounding her, the rainbow-coloured eyes of the horses, the purple glowing stare of the riders, the deadly long lances. But as one the horses fell to their knees and the riders flung down their weapons and covered their fair, terrible faces with their hair. Janet assumed, for a giddy instant, that they made obeisance out of respect for her courage. But out of the north came a grating cry like that of a night bird, and with its sound the horses flattened themselves upon the ground, and the riders shook with terror. The Great Queen had come.

Janet sat still as still, exhausted. She saw the terror of the riders but could not comprehend it. What person, what force, what power could bring such a host to its knees? Then, slowly, the circle of abject horses and riders parted, making a narrow gap, straight as an arrow towards the north road. Janet saw nothing, but felt in the furthest distance, as if beyond the northernmost north, the wheeling of a flock of black birds over ancient ice; the voice of a crow seemed to reach towards her and pass through her as if she was nothing, for it sought the man that she cradled in her arms, and had no other purpose but to reach him. It asked him how he had allowed a mere human to steal him back. But he slept, protected by Janet's mantle, warm and at peace.

Then the crow voice withdrew, and the prostrated army shuffled and reordered, the riders wrapping their long white hair ever tighter about their faces and moaning softly. An avenue opened to the south, and beyond the southernmost horizon Janet thought she saw a bush of green broom in full blossom, yet raging with consuming fire. From out of that bush came a warm, loving and deadly whisper: the Great Queen called upon her two sister-selves to witness this impudent theft of a life from her realm to that of mortal men. The golden murmur sunk into the ear of the sleeping man, but still he heard nothing.

When the voice died Janet began to wonder how they might fetch home to her father's hall, and knew that she would not be allowed to pass unscathed. Within the circle of the crossroads and beneath the guardian stone she was, briefly, safe, but she dare not step beyond the limit of the basins of milk and water. As she thought of this, she looked upon the basin that had held the water, and saw that it was dry. Next she looked upon the basin that had once held milk, now turned to blood.

Chess-piece – the Queen – with Celtic motifs.

As she looked the blood in that great basin seemed to drain away, as if taken in drink by an unseen presence. Then the eldritch army moaned and writhed and fell from their horses and covered their ears with their hands, pushing their faces into the horses' flanks to further muffle their hearing.

And from out of the west came the cry of a night owl, and within that the voice of a young girl. And again the voices passed through her towards the sleeping man. They sobbed and hooted and lilted that if they had known of such treachery as love, they would have plucked out his soft gentle brown eyes, and put in eyes from the knotty trunk of a hawthorn tree. And had they known of the power of the mortal heart, they would have torn his living heart from his body, and replaced it with a heart of granite stone.

And then the flock of crows, the burning flowering bush and the owl maiden rose up together and stretched their power towards the centre of the circle. The elfin horses screamed aloud, a tearing, desperate sound, and ran mad, kicking at their masters, and biting each other in the necks until clear green ichor flowed over the grass, which began to move and grow wherever the fluid touched.

The tall standing stone, with its tiny carving of the man, his arms outstretched in blessing, began to vibrate with the power of the Great Queen. Janet bent her head over the sleeper in her arms, and knew that when the stone shattered they would both die, at best, or at worst remain alive. She prayed for death, even if it was death for herself that he might stay alive and go free.

And with her prayer came a sudden hush, and the presence of the Great Queen faltered, then snapped away suddenly. Janet remained still, her eyes tight shut, awaiting the next onslaught. She could no longer hear the screaming of demented horses or the terrified fairy warriors. But there came instead a faint chorus of birds in the distant wood behind her, heralding the light of dawn, passing down the eastern road towards her.

When Janet and Tam Lin returned to her father's hall that morning, they found a new chess game about to begin. The king, with an unusual display of good sense, named Tam Lin his tanist or successor, and ambled off to talk to the pigs.

Janet thought a while, then took it upon herself to secretly remove the queen pieces from each of the boards, at night, one at a time. Of course no one suspected her, and no one has solved the problem of how to play the game properly from that day to this.

Chess-piece – the King – with Celtic motifs.

134

10

the Wooing of Emer
(Ireland)

In 'The Wasting Sickness of Cuchulainn' (Chapter 5), we found the hero already married to Emer. This is the story of their meeting, but it contains a wealth of mythic material interwoven with the basic theme. Although the stories revolve around Cuchulainn, they are not his exclusive biographies, and many insights into legend, magic and pagan Celtic religion are also present.

The version reprinted here comes from *The Cuchulainn Saga*, edited by E. Hull, 1898.

PART I

THERE lived once upon a time a great and famous king in Emain Macha, whose name was Conchobar, son of Fachtna *fathach*. In his reign there was much store of good things enjoyed by the men of Ulster. Peace there was, and quiet, and pleasant greeting; there were fruits and fatness and harvest of the sea; there was sway and law and good lordship during his time among the men of Erin. In the king's house at Emain was great state and rank and plenty. On this wise was that house, the Red Branch of Conchobar, namely, after the likeness of the house of Tara's Meadhall. Nine compartments were in it from the fire to the wall. Thirty feet was the height of each bronze partition that was in the house. Carvings of red yew therein. A wooden ceiling beneath and a roofing of tiles above. The compartment of Conchobar was in the forefront of the house, with ceilings of silver with pillars of bronze. Their headpieces glittering with gold and set with carbuncles, so that day and night were equally light therein, with its plate of silver above the king to the roof-tree of the royal house. Whenever Conchobar struck the plate with his royal rod, all the men of Ulster were silent. The twelve divisions of the twelve chariot-chiefs were round about the king's compartment. Yea all the valiant warriors of the men of Ulster found space in that king's house at the time of drinking, and yet no man of them would press upon the other. Splendid, lavish and beautiful were the valiant warriors of the men of Ulster in that house. In it were held great and numerous gatherings of every kind, and wonderful pastimes. Games and music and singing there, heroes performing their feats, poets singing, harpers and players on the *timpan* striking up their sounds.

Now, once the men of Ulster were in Emain Macha with Conchobar, drinking out of *iern-gual*. A hundred fillings of beverage went into it every evening. Such was the drinking of the *iern-gual*, which at one sitting would satisfy all the men of Ulster. The chariot-chiefs of Ulster were performing on ropes stretched across from door to door in the house at Emania. Fifteen feet and nine score was the size of that house. The chariot-chiefs were performing three feats, viz., the spear-feat, the apple-feat, and the sword-edge feat. The chariot-chiefs who performed those feats are these: Conall the Victorious, son of Amargin; Fergus, son of Rôich, the Over-bold; Laegaire the Triumphant, son of Conna; Celtchar, son of Uitechar; Dubhtach, son of Lugaid; Cúchulainn, son of Sualtach; Scel, son of Barnene (from whom the Pass of Barnene is named), the warder of Emain Macha. From him is the saying ' a story of Scel's', for he was a mighty story-teller. Cùchulainn surpassed them all at those feats for quickness and deftness. The women of Ulster loved Cúchulainn greatly for his dexterity in the feats, for the nimbleness of his leap, for the excellency of his wisdom, for the sweetness of his speech, for the beauty of his face, for the loveliness of his look. For in his kingly eyes were seven pupils, four of them in his one eye, and three of them in the other. He had seven fingers on either hand, and seven toes on either of his two feet. Many were his gifts. First, his gift of prudence until his warrior's flame appeared, the gift of feats, the gifts of *buanfach* (a game like chess or draughts), the gift of draught-playing, the gift of calculating, the gift of sooth-saying, the gift of discernment, the gift of beauty. But Cúchulainn had three defects: that he was too young, and all the more would unknown youths deride him, that he was too daring and that he was too beautiful. The men of Ulster took counsel about Cúchulainn, for their women and maidens loved him greatly. For Cúchulainn had no wife at that time. This was their counsel, that they should seek out a maiden whom Cúchulainn might choose to woo. For they were sure that a man who had a wife to attend to would less spoil their daughters and accept the love of their women. And, besides, they were troubled and afraid that Cúchulainn would perish early, so that for

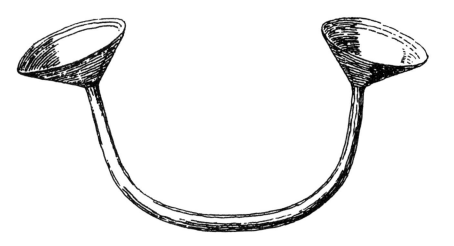

Ring with flower-calyx or trumpet terminals.

that reason they wished to give him a wife that he might leave an heir; knowing that his rebirth would be of himself.

Then Conchobar sent out nine men into each province of Erin to seek a wife for Cúchulainn, to see if in any dún, or in any chief-place in Erin, they could find the daughter of a king, or of a chief, or of a hospitaller, whom it might please Cúchulainn to woo.

All the messengers returned that day a year gone, and had not found a maiden whom Cúchulainn chose to woo. Thereupon Cúchulainn himself went to woo a maiden that he knew in Luglochta Loga, 'the Gardens of Lugh', namely, Emer, the daughter of Forgall the Wily. Cúchulainn himself, and his charioteer Laegh, son of Riangabar, went in his chariot. That was the one chariot which the host of the horses of the chariots of Ulster could not follow, on account of the swiftness and speed of the chariot, and of the chariot chief who sat in it. Then Cúchulainn found the maiden on her playing-field, with her foster-sisters around her, daughters of the land-owners that lived around the dún of Forgall. They were learning needlework and fine handiwork for Emer. Of all the maidens of Erin, she was the one maiden whom he deigned to address and to woo. For she had the six gifts: the gift of beauty, the gift of voice, the gift of sweet speech, the gift of needlework, the gifts of wisdom and chastity. Cúchulainn had said that no maiden should go with him but she who was his equal in age and form and race, in skill and deftness, who was the best handiworker of the maidens of Erin, for that none but such as she were a fitting wife for him. Now, as Emer was the one maiden who fulfilled all these conditions, Cúchulainn went to woo her above all.

It was in his festal array that Cúchulainn went forth that day to address Emer, and to show his beauty to her. As the maidens were sitting on the bench of gathering at the dún, they heard coming towards them

137

the clatter of horses' hoofs, with the creaking of the chariot, the cracking of straps, the grating of wheels, the rush of the hero, the clanking of weapons.

'Let one of you see,' said Emer, 'what it is that is coming towards us.'

'Truly, I see,' said Fiall, daughter of Forgall, 'two steeds alike in size, beauty, fierceness and speed, bounding side by side. Spirited they are and powerful, pricking their ears: their manes long and curling, and with curling tails. At the right side of the pole of the chariot is a grey horse, broad in the haunches, fierce, swift, wild; thundering he comes along, taking small bounds, with head erect and chest expanded. Beneath his four hard hoofs the firm and solid turf seems aflame. A flock of swift birds follows, but, as he takes his course along the road, a flash of breath darts from him, a blast of ruddy flaming sparks is poured from his curbed jaws.

'The other horse jet-black, his head firmly knit, his feet broad-hoofed and slender. Long and curly are his mane and tail. Down his broad forehead hang heavy curls of hair. Spirited and fiery, he fiercely strides along, stamping firmly on the ground. Beautiful he sweeps along as having outstripped the horses of the land; he bounds over the smooth dry sward, following the levels of the mid-glen, where no obstacle obstructs his pace.

'I see a chariot of fine wood with wicker-work, moving on wheels of white bronze. A pole of white silver, with a mounting of white bronze. Its frame very high of creaking copper, rounded and firm. A strong curved yoke of gold. Two firm plaited yellow reins. The shafts hard and straight as sword-blades.

'Within the chariot a dark sad man, comeliest of the men of Erin. Around him a beautiful crimson five-folded tunic, fastened at its opening on his white breast with a brooch of inlaid gold, against which it heaves, beating in full strokes. A shirt with a white hood, interwoven red with flaming gold. Seven red dragon-gems on the ground of either of his eyes. Two blue-white, blood-red cheeks that breathe forth sparks and flashes of fire. A ray of love burns in his look. Methinks, a shower of pearls has fallen into his mouth. As black as the side of a black ruin each of his eyebrows. On his two thighs rests a golden-hilted sword, and fastened to the copper frame of the chariot is a blood-red spear with a sharp mettlesome blade, on a shaft of wood well fitted to the hand. Over his shoulders a crimson shield with a rim of silver, ornamented with figures of golden animals. He leaps the hero's salmon-leap into the air, and does many like swift feats. . . the chariot-chief of the single chariot.

'Before him in that chariot there is a charioteer, a very slender, tall, much-freckled man. On his head is very curly bright-red hair, a fillet of bronze upon his brow which prevents the hair from falling over his face. On both sides of his head clasps of gold confine the hair. A shoulder mantle about him with sleeves opening at the two elbows, and in his hand a goad of red gold with which he guides the horses.'

Meanwhile, Cúchulainn had come to the place where the maidens were. And he wished a blessing to them.

Emer lifted up her lovely face and recognized Cúchulainn, and she said, 'May God make smooth the path before you!'

'And you,' he said, 'may you be safe from every harm!'

'Whence comest thou?' she asked.

'From Intide Emna,' he replied.

'Where did you sleep?' said she.

'We slept,' he said, 'in the house of the man who tends the cattle of the plain of Tethra.'

'What was your food there?' she asked.

'The ruin of a chariot was cooked for us there,' he replied.

'Which way didst thou come?'

'Between the Two Mountains of the Wood,' said he.

'Which way didst thou take after that?'

'That is not hard to tell,' he said. 'From the Cover of the Sea, over the Great Secret of the Tuatha dé Danann, and the Foam of the two steeds of Emania; over the Morrigan's Garden, and the Great Sow's Back; over the Glen of the Great Dam, between the god and his prophet; over the Marrow of the Woman Fedelm, between the boar and his dam; over the Washing-place of the horses of Dea; between the King of Ana and his servant, to Mondchuile of the Four Corners of the World; over Great Crime and the Remnants of the Great Feast; between the Vat and the Little Vat, to the Gardens of Lugh, to the daughters of Tethra's nephew, Forgall the King of the Fomori. And what, o maiden, is the account of thee?' said Cúchulainn.

'Truly, that is not hard to tell,' said the maiden. 'Tara of the women, whitest of maidens, the flower of chastity, a prohibition that is not taken, a watcher that sees no one. A modest woman is a worm, . . . a rush which none comes near. The daughter of a king is a flame of hospitality, a road that cannot be entered. I have champions that follow me to guard me from whoever would carry me off against their will, without their and Forgall's knowledge of my act.'

'Who are the champions that follow thee, o maiden?' said Cúchulainn.

'Truly, it is not hard to tell,' said Emer. 'Two called Lui, two Luaths; Luath and Lath Goible, son of Tethra; Traith and Trescath, Brion and Bolor; Bas, son of Omnach; eight called Condla; and Cond, son of Forgall. Every man of them has the strength of a hundred and the feats of nine. Hard it were too to tell the many powers of Forgall's self. He is stronger than any labourer, more learned than any druid, more acute than any poet. It will be more than all your games to fight against Forgall himself. For many powers of his have been recounted of manly deeds.'

'Why dost thou not reckon me, o maiden, with those strong men?' said Cúchulainn.

'If thy deeds have been recounted, why should I not reckon thee among them?'

'Truly, I swear, o maiden,' said Cúchulainn, 'that I shall make my deeds to be recounted among the glories of the strength of heroes.'

'What, then, is thy strength?' said Emer.

'That is quickly told,' said he. 'When my strength in fight is weakest, I defend twenty. A third part of my strength is sufficient for thirty. Alone, I make combat against forty. Under my protection a hundred are secure. From dread of me, warriors avoid fords and battlefields. Hosts and multitudes and many armed men flee before the terror of my face.'

'Those are goodly fights for a tender boy,' said the maiden, 'But thou hast not yet reached the strength of chariot-chiefs.'

'Truly, o maiden,' said he, 'well have I been brought up by my dear

Pictish pattern on shield.

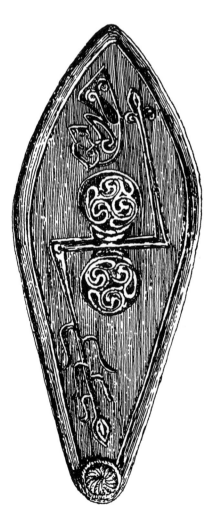

foster-father Conchobar. Not as a churl looks to the heritage of his children, between flag and kneading-trough, between fire and wall, nor on the floor of the single larder have I been brought up by Conchobar; but among chariot-chiefs and champions, among jesters and druids, among poets and learned men, among the lords of land and farmers of Ulster have I been reared, so that I have all their manners and gifts.'

'Who then were they who brought thee up on all those deeds of which thou boastest?' said Emer.

'That, truly, were easily told. Fair-speeched Sencha has taught me, so that I am strong, wise, swift, deft. I am prudent in judgement, my memory is good. Before wise men, I make answer to many; I give heed to their arguments. I direct the judgements of all the men of Ulster, and, through the training of Sencha, my decisions are unalterable.

'Blai, the lord of lands, on account of his racial kinship, took me to himself, so that I got my due with him. I invite the men of Conchobar's province with their king. I entertain them for the space of a week, I settle their gifts and their spoils, I aid them in their honour and their fines.

'Fergus has so fostered me that I slay mighty warriors through the strength of valour. I am fierce in might and in prowess, so that I am able to guard the borders of the land against foreign foes. I am a shelter for every poor man, I am a rampart of fight for every wealthy man; I give comfort to him who is wretched, I deal out mischief to him who is strong: all this through the fosterage of Fergus.

'Amargin the poet, to his knee I came. Therefore I am able to praise a king for the possession of any excellency; therefore I can stand up to any man in valour, in prowess, in wisdom, in splendour, in cleverness, in justice, in boldness. I am a match for any chariot-chief. I yield thanks to none, save Conchobar the Battle-Victorious.

'Finnchoem has reared me, so that Conall *cernach* is my foster-brother.

'For the sake of Dechtire, Cathbad of the gentle face hath taught me, so that I am an adept in the arts of the god of druidism, and learned in the excellencies of knowledge.

'All the men of Ulster have taken part in my bringing-up, alike charioteers and chariot-chiefs, kings and chief poets, so that I am the darling of the host and multitude, so that I fight for the honour of them all alike.

'Honourably have I been asked by Lugh, son of Cond mac Ethlend . . . of Dechtire to the house . . . of the Brugh. And thou, o maiden,' said Cúchulainn, 'how has thou been reared in the Gardens of Lugh?'

'It is not hard to relate that to thee, truly,' answered the maiden. 'I was brought up,' said she, 'in ancient virtues, in lawful behaviour, in the keeping of chastity, in rank equal to a queen, in stateliness of form, so that to me is attributed every noble grace of form among the hosts of Erin's women.'

'Good indeed are those virtues,' said Cúchulainn. 'Why, then, should it not be fitting for us both to become one? For I have not hitherto found a maiden capable of holding converse with me at a meeting in this wise.'

'Yet one question,' said the maiden. 'Hast thou a wife already?'

'Not so,' said Cúchulainn.

Said the maiden, 'I may not marry before my sister is married, for she is older than I; namely, Fial, daughter of Forgall, whom thou seest with me here. She is excellent in handiwork.'

'It is not she, truly, with whom I have fallen in love,' said Cúchulainn. 'Nor have I ever accepted a woman who has known a man before me, and I have been told that yon girl was once Cairpre *naifer*'s.'

While they were thus conversing, Cúchulainn saw the breasts of the maiden over the bosom of her smock. And he said: 'Fair is this plain, the plain of the noble yoke.'

Then the maiden spake these words: 'No one comes to this plain, who does not slay as many as a hundred on such ford from the Ford of Scennmenn at Ollbine to Banchuing Arcait, where swift Brea breaks the brow of Fedelm.'

'Fair is this plain, the plain of the noble yoke,' said Cúchulainn.

'No one comes to this plain,' said she, 'who has not achieved the feat of slaying three times nine men at one blow, o calf of the cow, . . . yet so as to preserve one man in the midst of each nine of them alive.'

'Fair is this plain, the plain of the noble yoke,' said Cùchulainn.

'None comes to this plain,' said she, 'who does not, from summer's end to the beginning of spring, from the beginning of spring to May-day, and again from May-day to the beginning of winter meet Benn Suian, son of Roscmelc.'

'Even as thou hast commanded, so shall all by me be done,' said Cúchulainn.

'And by me thy offer is accepted, it is taken, it is granted,' said Emer. 'Yet one question more. What is thy account of thyself?' said she.

'I am the nephew of the man that disappears in another in the wood of Badb,' said he.

'And thy name?' she said. 'I am the hero of the plague that befalls dogs,' said he.

After those notable words, Cúchulainn went from thence, and they did not hold any further converse on that day.

While Cúchulainn was driving across Bregia, Laegh, his charioteer, asked him: 'Now,' said he, 'the words that thou and the maiden Emer spoke, what didst thou mean by them?'

'Dost thou not know,' answered Cúchulainn, 'that I am wooing Emer? And it is for this reason that we disguised our words lest the girls should understand that I am wooing her. For, if Forgall knew it, we should not meet with his consent.'

Cúchulainn then repeated the conversation from the beginning to his charioteer, explaining it to him, to beguile the length of their way.

Cúchulainn went driving on his way, and slept that night in Emain Macha.

Then their daughters told the land-owners of the youth that had come in his splendid chariot, and of the conversation held between him and Emer: that they did not know what they said to one another; and that he had turned from them across the plain of Bregia northward.

Then the lords of land relate all this to Forgall the Wily, and tell him that the girl had spoken to Cúchulainn. 'It is true,' said Forgall the Wily. 'The madman from Emain Macha has been here to converse with Emer, and the girl has fallen in love with him: that is why they talked one to another. But it shall avail them nothing. I shall hinder them,' he said.

Thereupon Forgall the Wily went towards Emain Macha in the garb of a foreigner, as if it were an embassy from the king of the Gauls that had come to confer with Conchobar, with an offering to him of golden treasures, and wine of Gaul, and all sorts of good things besides. In number they were three.

Great welcome was made to him. When on the third day he had sent away his men Cúchulainn and Conall and other chariot-chiefs of Ulster were praised before him. He said that it was true, that the chariot-chiefs performed marvellously, but that were Cúchulainn to go to Donall the Brave from Alba, his skill would be more wonderful still; and that if he went to Scathach to learn soldierly feats, he would excel the warriors of all Europe.

But the reason for which he proposed this to Cúchulainn was that he might never return again. For he thought that if Cúchulainn became her friend, he would come to his death thereby, through the wildness and fierceness of yonder warrior. Cúchulainn consented to go, and Forgall bound himself to give Cúchulainn whatever he desired, if he should go within a certain time.

Forgall went home, and the warriors arose in the morning and set themselves to do as they had vowed.

So they started; Cúchulainn and Laegaire the Triumphant, and Conchobar; and Conall *cernach*, some say, went with them. But Cúchulainn first went across the plain of Bray to visit the maiden. He talked to Emer before going in the ship, and the maiden told him that it had been Forgall, who in Emania had desired him to go and learn soldierly feats, in order that they two might not meet. And she bade him be on his guard wherever he went, lest Forgall should destroy him. Either of them promised the other to keep their chastity until they should meet again, unless either of them died meanwhile. They bade each other farewell, and he turned towards Alba.

PART II

Cúchulainn's education in championship

When they reached Donall, they were taught by him to blow a leathern bellows under the flagstone of the small hole. On it they would perform till their soles were black or livid. They were taught another thing on a spear, on which they would jump and perform on its point; this was called 'the champion's coiling round the points of spears' or 'dropping on its head'.

Then the daughter of Donall, Big-Fist by name, fell in love with Cúchulainn. Her form was very gruesome, her knees were large, her heels turned before her, her feet behind her; big dark-grey eyes in her head, her face as black as a bowl of jet. A very large forehead she had, her rough bright-red hair in threads wound round her head. Cúchulainn refused her. Then she swore to be revenged on him for this.

Donall said that Cúchulainn would not have perfect knowledge of their learning until he went to Scathach, who lived to the east of Alba. So the four went across Alba, viz., Cúchulainn and Conchobar, King of Ulster, and Conall *cernach*, and Laegaire the Triumphant. Then before their eyes appeared unto them in a vision Emain Macha, past which Conchobar and Conall and Laegaire were not able to go. The daughter of Donall had raised that vision in order to sever Cúchulainn from his companions to his ruin. Other versions say, that it was Forgall the Wily who raised this vision before them to induce them to turn back, so that by returning Cúchulainn should fail to fulfil what he had promised him in Emania, and thereby he would be shamed; or that were he peradventure in spite of it to go eastward to learn soldierly feats, both known and unknown, of Aife, he should be still more likely to be killed, being alone. Then, of his own free will, Cúchulainn departed from them along an unknown road, for the powers of the girl were great, and she wrought evil against him, and severed him from his companions.

Now, when Cúchulainn went across Alba, he was sad and gloomy and weary for the loss of his comrades, neither knew he whither he should go to seek Scathach. For he had promised his comrades that he would not return again to Emain, unless he either reached Scathach or met his death.

He now, seeing that he was astray and ignorant, lingered; and while he was there, he beheld a terrible great beast like a lion coming towards him, which kept watching him, but did not do him any harm. Whichever way he went, the beast went before him, turning its side towards him. Then he took a leap and was on its back. He did not guide it, but went wherever the beast liked. In that wise they journeyed four days, until they came to the uttermost bounds of men, and to an island where lads

were rowing on a small loch. The lads laughed at the unwonted sight of
the hurtful beast doing service to a man. Cúchulainn then leaped off, and
the beast parted from him, and he bade it farewell.

He passed on, and came to a large house in a deep glen, wherein was
a maiden fair of form. The maiden addressed him, and bade him welcome.
'Welcome thy coming, o Cúchulainn!' said she. He asked her how she
knew him. She answered that they both had been dear foster-children
with Wulfkin the Saxon, 'when I was there, and thou learning sweet
speech from him,' said she. She then gave him meat and drink and he
turned away from her. Then he met a brave youth who gave him the
same welcome. They conversed together, and Cúchulainn enquired of
him the way to the dún of Scathach. The youth taught him the way
across the Plain of Ill-luck that lay before him. On the hither half of the
plain the feet of men would stick fast; on the farther half the grass would
rise and hold them fast on the points of its blades. The youth gave him
a wheel, and told him to follow its track across one half of the plain. He
gave him also an apple, and told him to follow the way along which the
apple ran, and that in such wise he would reach the end of the plain.
Thus Cúchulainn eventually did go across the plain; afterwards
proceeding farther on. The youth had told him that there was a large glen
before him, and a single narrow path through it, which was full of
monsters that had been sent by Forgall to destroy him, and that his road
to the house of Scathach lay across terrible high, strong mountain
fastnesses. Then each of them wished a blessing to the other, Cúchulainn
and the youth Eochu *bairche*. It was he who taught him how he should
win honour in the house of Scathach. The same youth also foretold to
him what he would suffer of hardships and straits in the Táin Bó

Cuailgne, and what evil and exploits and contests he would achieve against the men of Erin.

Then Cúchulainn, following the young man's instructions, went on that road across the Plain of Ill-luck and through the Perilous Glen. This was the road that Cúchulainn took to the camp where the scholars of Scathach were. He asked where she was.

'In yonder island,' said he.

'Which way must I take to reach her,' said he.

'By the Bridge of the Cliff,' say they, 'which no man can cross until he has achieved valour.' For on this wise was that bridge. It had two low ends and the mid-space high, and whenever anybody leaped on one end of it, the other head would lift itself up and throw him on his back. Some versions relate that a crowd of the warriors of Erin were in that dún learning feats from Scathach, namely, Ferdia son of Daman, and Naisi son of Usnach, and Loch *mór* son of Egomos, and Fiamain son of Fora, and an innumerable host besides. But in this version it is not told that they were there at that time.

Cúchulainn tried three times to cross the bridge and could not do it. The men jeered at him. Then he grew mad, and jumped upon the head of the bridge, and made 'the hero's salmon-leap', so that he landed on the middle of it; and the other head of the bridge had not fully raised itself up when he reached it, and threw himself from it, and was on the ground of the island.

He went up to the dún, and struck the door with the shaft of his spear, so that it went through it. Scathach was told, 'Truly,' said she, 'this must be some one who has achieved valour elsewhere.' And she sent her daughter Uathach to know who the youth might be . . .

Then Uathach came and conversed with Cúchulainn. On the third day she advised him, if it were to achieve valour that he had come, that he should go though the hero's salmon-leap to reach Scathach, in the place where she was teaching her two sons, Cuar and Cett, in the great yew-tree; that he should set his sword between her breasts until she yielded him his three wishes: namely, to teach him without neglect; that without the payment of wedding-gifts he might wed Uathach; and that she should foretell his future, for she was a prophetess.

Cúchulainn then went to the place where Scathach was. He placed his two feet on the two edges of the basket of the *cless*, and bared his sword, and put its point to her heart, saying, 'Death hangs over thee!'

'Name thy three demands!' said she; 'thy three demands, as thou canst utter them in one breath.'

'They must be fulfilled,' said Cúchulainn. And he pledged her . . . Uathach then was given to Cúchulainn, and Scathach taught him skill of arms.

During the time that he was with Scathach, and was the husband of Uathach her daughter, a certain famous man who lived in Munster, by name Lugaid son of Nos son of Alamac, the renowned king and foster-brother of Cúchulainn, went eastwards with twelve chariot-chiefs of the high kings of Munster, to woo twelve maidens of the men of Mac Rossa, but they had all been betrothed before.

When Forgall the Wily heard this, he went to Tara, and told Lugaid that the best maiden in Erin, both as to form and chastity and handiwork, was in his house unmarried. Lugaid said it pleased him well. Then Forgall betrothed the maiden to the king; and to the twelve under-kings that were together with Lugaid, he betrothed twelve daughters of twelve landed proprietors in Bregia.

The king accompanied Forgall to his dún for the wedding.

When now Emer was brought to Lugaid, to sit by his side, she took between both her hands his two cheeks, and laid it on the truth of his honour and his life, confessing that it was Cúchulainn she loved, that Forgall was against it, and that any one who should take her as his wife would suffer loss of honour. Then, for fear of Cúchulainn, Lugaid did not dare to take Emer, and so returned home again.

Scatach was at that time carrying on war against other tribes, over whom the Princess Aife ruled. The two hosts assembled to fight, but Cúchulainn had been put in bonds by Scathach, and a sleeping-potion given him beforehand to prevent him going into the battle, lest anything should befall him there. But, after an hour, Cúchulainn suddenly started out of his sleep. This sleeping-potion, that would have anybody else for twenty-four hours in sleep, held him only for one hour. He went forth with the two sons of Scathach against the three sons of Ilsuanach, namely, Cuar, Cett and Cruife, three warriors of Aife's. Alone he encountered them all three, and they fell by him. On the next morning again the battle was set, and the two hosts marched forward until the two lines met, face to face. Then the three sons of Ess Enchenn advanced, namely, Cire, Bire and Blaicne, three other of Aife's warriors, and began to combat against the two sons of Scathach. They went on the path of feats. Thereupon Scathach uttered a sigh, for she knew not what would come of it; first, because there was no third man with her two sons against those three, and next, because she was afraid of Aife, who was the hardest woman-warrior in the world. Cúchulainn, however, went up to her two sons, and sprang upon the path, and met all three, and they fell by him.

Aife then challenged Scathach to combat, and Cúchulainn went forth to meet Aife. Before going he asked what it was Aife loved most. Scathach said: 'What most she loves are her two horses, her chariot, and her charioteer.' Cúchulainn and Aife went to the path of feats, and began combat there. Aife shattered Cúchulainn's weapon, and his sword was broken off at the hilt. Then Cúchulainn cried: 'Ah me, the charioteer of Aife, her two horses, and her chariot have fallen down the glen, and all have perished!' At that Aife looked up.

Then Cúchulainn went up to her, seized her under her two breasts, took her on his back like a shoulder-load, and bore her away to his own host. Then he threw her from him to the ground, and over her held his naked sword.

'Life for life, o Cúchulainn!' said Aife.

'My three demands to me!' said he.

'Thou shalt have them as thou breathest them,' she said.

'These are my three demands,' he said. 'that thou give hostage to Scathach, nor ever afterwards oppose her, that thou remain with me this night before thy dún, and that thou bear me a son.'

'I promise all this to thee,' said she.

And in this wise it was done. Cúchulainn went with Aife and remained with her that night. Then Aife said she was with child, and that she would bear a boy. 'On this day seven years I will send him to Erin,' she said, 'and leave thou a name for him.' Cúchulainn left a golden finger-ring for him, and told her that the boy was to go and seek him in Erin, so soon as the ring should fit on his finger. And he said that Conla was the name to be given him, and charged her that he should not make himself known to any: also, that he should not turn out of the way of any man; nor refuse combat to any. Thereupon Cúchulainn returned back again to his own people.

As he went along the same road, he met an old woman on the road, blind of her left eye. She asked him to beware, and to avoid the road before her. He said there was no other footing for him, save on the cliff of the sea that was beneath him. She besought him to leave the road to her. Then he left the road, only clinging to it with his toes. As she passed over him she hit his great toe to throw him off the path, down the cliff. He noticed it, and leapt the hero's salmon-leap up again, and struck off the woman's head. She was Ess Enchenn, the mother of the last three warriors that had fallen by him, and it was in order to destroy him that she had come to meet him.

After that the hosts returned with Scathach to her own land, and hostages were given to her by Aife. And Cúchulainn stayed there for the day of his recovery.

At last, when the full lore of soldierly arts with Scathach had been mastered by Cúchulainn – as well the apple-feat as the thunder-feat, the blade-feat, the supine-feat, and the spear-feat, the rope-feat, the body-feat, the cat's-feat, the salmon-feat of a chariot-chief; the throw of the staff, the whirl of a brave chariot-chief, the spear of the *gae bulga*, the *boi* of swiftness, the wheel-feat, the *othar* feat, the breath-feat, the *brud geme*, the hero's whoop, the blow... the counter-blow; running up a lance and righting the body on its point; the scythe-chariot, and the hero's twisting round spear points – then came to him a message to return to his own land and he took his leave.

Then Scathach told him what would befall him in the future, and sang to him in the seer's large shining ken, and spake these words:

Welcome, o victorious, warlike ...
At the Lifting of the Kine of Bray,
Thou wilt be a chariot-chief in single combat.
Great peril awaits thee ...
Alone against a vast herd ...
The warriors of Cruachan, thou wilt scatter them.
Thy name shall reach the men of Alba ...
Thirty years I reckon the strength of thy valour.
Further than this I do not add.

Then Cúchulainn went on board his ship, to set out for Erin. These were the voyagers in the ship: Lugaid and Luan, the two sons of Lôch; Ferbaeth, Larin, Ferdia, and Durst son of Serb. They came to the house of Ruad, king of the Isles, on Samhain night. Conall *cernach*, and Laegaire *buadach* 'The Triumphant', were there before them, levying tribute; for at that time a tribute was paid to Ulster from the Isles of the Foreigners.

Then Cúchuliann heard sounds of wailing before him in the dún of the king.

'What is that lamentation?' asked Cúchulainn.

'It is because the daughter of Ruad is given as tribute to the Fomori,' said they.

'Where is the maiden?' he said.

They answered, 'She is on the shore below.'

Cúchulainn went down to the strand, and drew near to the maiden. He asked her the meaning of her plight, and she told him fully.

Seventeenth-century powder horn with Celtic triple knot, Scottish Highlands.

Said he, 'Whence do the men come?'

'From that distant land yonder. Remain not here,' she said, 'in sight of the robbers.'

But he remained there awaiting them, and he killed the three Fomori in single combat. The last man wounded him in the wrist, and the maiden gave him a strip from her garment to bind round his wound. Then he departed without making himself known to her. The maiden come to the dún, and told her father the whole story; and afterwards came Cúchulainn to the dún, like every other guest. Conall and Laegaire bade him welcome, and there were many in the dún who boasted of having slain the Fomori, but the maiden believed them not. Then the king had a bath prepared, and afterwards each one was brought to her separately. Cúchulainn came, like all the rest, and the maiden recognized him.

'I will give the maiden to thee,' said Ruad, ' and I myself will pay her wedding-dowry.'

'Not so,' said Cúchulainn. 'But if it please her, let her follow me this day year to Erin; there she will find me.'

Then Cúchulainn came to Emain and related all his adventures. When he had cast his fatigue from him he set out to seek Emer at the rath of Forgall. For a whole year he remained near it, but could not approach her for the number of the watch.

At the end of the year he came and said to his charioteer, 'It is today, o Laegh, that we have our tryst with the daughter of Raud, but we know not the exact place, for we were not wise. Let us go to the coast.'

When they came to the shore of Loch Cuan [Strangford Lough], they beheld two birds on the sea. Cúchulainn put a stone in his sling, and aimed at the birds. The men ran up to them, after having hit one of the birds. When they came up to them, lo! they saw two women, the most beautiful in the world. They were Dervorgil, the daughter of Ruad, and her handmaid.

'Evil is the deed that thou hast done, o Cúchulainn,' said she. 'It was to meet thee we came, and now thou hast hurt us.'

Cúchulainn sucked the stone out of her, with its clot of blood round it. 'I cannot wed thee now,' said Cúchuliann, 'for I have drunk thy blood. But I will give thee to my companion here, Lugaid, of the Red Stripes.' And so it was done.

Then Cúchulainn desired to go to the rath of Forgall. And that day the scythe-chariot was prepared for him. It was called the scythe-chariot on account of the iron scythes that stood out from it, or, perhaps, because it was first invented by the Serians. When he arrived at the rath of Forgall, he jumped the hero's salmon-leap across the three ramparts, so that he was on the ground of the dún. And he dealt three blows in the liss, so that eight men fell from each blow, and one escaped in each group of nine, namely, Scibur, Ibur, and Cat, three brothers of Emer.

Forgall made a leap on to the rampart of the rath without, fleeing from Cúchulainn, and he fell lifeless. The Cúchulainn carried off Emer, and her foster-sister, with their two loads of gold and silver, leaping back again across the third rampart, and so went forth.

From every direction cries were raised around them. Scennmend rushed against them. Cúchulainn killed her at the ford, hence called the ford of Scennmend. Thence they escaped to Glondáth, and there Cúchulainn killed a hundred of them.

'Great is the deed that thou hast done,' said Emer; 'to have killed a hundred armed able-bodied men.'

'Glond-áth, the ford of deeds, shall be its name for ever,' said Cúchulainn.

He reached Crúfoit 'Blood-turf', which until then had been called Rae-bán 'White Field'. He dealt great angry blows on the hosts in that place, so that streams of blood broke over it on every side.

'By thy work, the hill is covered with a blood-stained turf today, Cúchulainn,' cried the maiden. Hence it is called *Crúfoit* or Cró-fót, 'Turf of Blood'.

The pursuers overtook them at Ath n-Imfúait on the Boyne. Emer left the chariot, and Cúchulainn pursued them along the banks, the clods flying from the hoofs of the horses across the ford northward. Then he turned, and pursued them northward, so that the clods flew over the ford southward from the hoofs of the horses. Hence it is called the 'Ford of the Two Clods', from the flying of the sods hither and thither. Now at each ford, from Ath Scennmend at Ollbine to the Boyne of Bray, Cúchulainn killed a hundred, and so he fulfilled all the deeds that he had vowed to the maiden, and he came safely out of all, and reached Emain Macha towards the fall of night.

Emer was bought into the House of the Red Branch to Conchobar and to the men of Ulster, and they bade her welcome ... Cúchulainn then took to himself his wife, and thenceforward they were not separated until they died.

afterword

This book is only the beginning of a plunge into Celtic myths and legends. In the short Bibliography that follows I have listed a range of sources for further reading, and this is intentionally wide. I do not believe that the true spirit of Celtic legend is limited solely to academic translations or even to accurate rendition from oral tradition and folklore. Celtic tradition is also found by feeling, through an imaginative quality often confused with 'romance' or false sensitivity, but in truth earthy and vital. While accurate academic work in research and translation is of great value, we should also admit that new creations can occur within the wide range of Celtic myths and legends, and that this range can be extended into the next century.

bibliography

The first entry under each chapter title is the main source for the story (all stories have been selected, adapted or completely rewritten by R. J. Stewart). The books listed next are both relevant and carry extensive bibliographies, and then there is a separate section of Further Reading.

1 Bran and Branwen

The Mabinogion, translated by Lady Charlotte Guest (with notes by Alfred Nutt), Alfred Nutt, London, 1904.
See also
The Mabinogion, translated by J. Gantz, Penguin Books, Harmondsworth, 1976.
Mabon and the Mysteries of Britain, Caitlín Matthews, Arkana, London, 1987.

2 The Wooing of Etain

Ancient Irish Tales, translated by Tom Peete Cross and Clark Harris Slover, Holt, Dublin, 1936.

3 The Curse of Macha

This story has been adapted from various sources.
See also
The Serpent and the Cross, M. Condren, Harper and Row, San Francisco, 1990.

4 'I don't know': The Tale of N'oun-Doaré

Folk Tales of Brittany, M. Luzel, Paris, 1890 (translated and adapted by R. J. Stewart).

5 The Wasting Sickness of Cuchulainn

Ancient Irish Tales, translated by Tom Peete Cross and Clark Harris Slover, Holt, Dublin, 1936.

6 The Marriage of Sir Gawain

Thomas Percy: Reliques of Ancient English Poetry, 3 vols., 1765; Dent, London, n.d.
See also
Gawain, Knight of the Goddess, John Matthews, Aquarian Press, London, 1990.

7 The Warrior of the Red Shield

Popular Tales of the Western Highlands, J. F. Campbell, Edinburgh, 1860.

8 Merlin, Old and Young

The Prophetic Vision of Merlin, R. J. Stewart, Arkana, London, 1986 (includes translation of and commentary on the *Prophecies of Merlin* of 1135 by Geoffrey of Monmouth).
See also
History of the Kings of Britain, Geoffrey of Monmouth, edited by Lewis Thorpe, Penguin Books, Harmondsworth, 1966.
The Complete Merlin Tarot, R. J. Stewart, illustrated by Miranda Gray, Aquarian Press, Wellingborough, 1988 and 1991.
The Mystic Life of Merlin, R. J. Stewart, Arkana, London, 1987 (includes translation of and commentary on the *Vita Merlini* by Geoffrey of Monmouth).
The Way of Merlin, R. J. Stewart, Aquarian Press, London, 1991.

9 Tam Lin, or The Game of Chess

Magical Tales, R. J. Stewart, Aquarian Press, Wellingborough, 1990.
See also
Where is Saint George?, R. J. Stewart, Blandford, London, 1988 (pagan imagery in English folksong; reprint of the 1976 edition).
Folklore in the English and Scottish Ballads, L. C. Wimberley, Frederick Ungar, New York, 1959.
The Fairy Faith in Celtic Countries, W. Y. Evans Wentz, Oxford, 1911.

10 The Wooing of Emer

The Cuchulainn Saga, edited by E. Hull, London, 1898.
See also
Cuchulainn, R. J. Stewart, Firebird Books, Poole, 1988.

Further Reading

Bromwich, R., *The Welsh Traids*, Cardiff University Press, 1961.
Caesar, Julius, *The Conquest of Gaul*, translated by S. A. Handford, Penguin Books, Harmondsworth, 1963.
Calder, G. (ed.), *The Scholar's Primer*, Edinburgh, 1917.
Cunliffe, B., *The Celtic World*, The Bodley Head, London, 1979.
Dillon, M. and N. Chadwick, *The Celtic Realms*, Weidenfeld and Nicolson, New York, 1967.
Eliade, M., *Shamanism: Archaic Techniques of Ecstasy*, translated by W. Trask, Arkana, Harmondsworth, 1989.
Fell, B., *America BC: Ancient Settlers in the New World*, Pocket Books, New York, 1976.
Geoffrey of Monmouth, *History of the Kings of Britain*, various translations.
Giraldus Cambrensis, *The History and Topography of Ireland*, various translations (recent: L. Thorpe, Penguin Books, Harmondsworth, 1982).
Graves, R., *The White Goddess*, Faber and Faber, London, 1975.
Mac Cana, P., *Celtic Mythology*, Hamlyn, London, 1975.
Matthews, J. and C., *The Aquarian Guide to British and Irish Mythology*, Aquarian Press, Wellingborough, 1988.
Matthews, J. and R. J. Stewart, *Warriors of Arthur*, Blandford, London, 1987.
Legendary Britain, Blandford, London, 1989.

Piggot, S., *The Druids*, Penguin Books, Harmondsworth, 1968.

The Quest of the Holy Grail, translated by P. J. Matarasso, Penguin Books, Harmondsworth, 1969.

Rees, A. and B., *Celtic Heritage*, Thames and Hudson, London, 1961.

Ross, A., *Pagan Celtic Britain*, Cardinal, London, 1974.

Stewart, R. J., *The Waters of the Gap*, Bath City Council, 1980; second edition Ashgrove/Gateway, Bath, 1989.

Stewart, R. J., *Celtic Gods, Celtic Goddesses*, Blandford, London, 1990.

Tatlock, J. S. P., *The Legendary History of Britain*, University of California Press, Berkeley, 1950.

Index